## Praise for *Building Your Business the Right-Brain Way*

"Who says creatives don't have the analytical skills to make it as entrepreneurs? Jennifer Lee's new book shows you how to put your right-brain strengths to work in a successful business, and does it in a way that's playful and fun. And don't worry — she includes frequent check-ins with your analytical side to make sure you're staying on track."
— Daniel H. Pink, *New York Times* bestselling author of · *To Sell Is Human* and *A Whole New Mind*

"If having a business plan is like planting a seed, implementing that plan is where you harvest the fruit. This book provides the sun, rain, shade, and soil to grow a healthy and fun, profitable and creative business."
— Andrea J. Lee, CEO of Wealthy Thought Leader

"Once again, Jennifer Lee has breathed life, color, and creativity into a business book, making it instantly enjoyable and relevant for the huge part of our population who does not relate to dry, academic approaches to growing a business. This book is written as an experience, with insanely practical applications that will grow your business."
— Pamela Slim, bestselling author of *Body of Work*

"It's a well-kept secret, but it's true: creative people can make terrific entrepreneurs. At least, they can once someone shows them how to do it and still have fun. Cheerful, practical, and wise, Jennifer Lee's ingenious book demystifies the cold, foreboding world of 'business' and gives unconventional people ways to develop a creative enterprise that is profitable, flexible, and brimming with personality. I can't wait to share this book!"
— Sam Bennett, author of *Get It Done*

"This fabulous book is a gift to the creative community. It's exactly the kind of book I would have loved when I started out. It shows creative people how to make a good living, and is full of pictures and playful worksheets, which makes it fun — and fun is key."
— Lilla Rogers, artists' agent and author of *I Just Like to Make Things*

"With plucky and practical guidance, Jennifer Lee is back again to inspire the new wave of creative entrepreneurs. This book goes beyond sharing why creative people can be great businesspeople and offers guidance in how to do it. *Building Your Business the Right-Brain Way* strikes the right balance between contemporary business-building advice and creative, colorful fun."    — Marney K. Makridakis, author of *Creating Time* and founder of ArtellaLand.com

"Fully absorbing *Building Your Business the Right-Brain Way* will give you the confidence to take risks, take action, and take control of your future. Think big."

— from the foreword by Michael Port, *New York Times* bestselling author of *Book Yourself Solid ILLUSTRATED*

"There is no magic formula to owning and operating a successful creative business. The best course of action is to always stay true to yourself, do what feels best to you, and gather support and community around your big dream. Jennifer Lee shows us how to do just that. You'll walk away from this book feeling empowered, motivated, and ready to accomplish your biggest creative business goals."

— Kari Chapin, author of *The Handmade Marketplace*

## Praise for Jennifer Lee's *The Right-Brain Business Plan*

"Lee's illustrated, colorful worksheets and step-by-step instructions are playful yet practical, transforming drudgery into joy."    — *Aznet News*

"Through her writing and the many fanciful illustrations, Lee demonstrates that producing a business plan can indeed be a creative endeavor. While the book covers all the basics of how to put together a business plan, something found in several other competing titles, getting to the end product will likely be a lot more fun with Lee's approach."    — *ForeWord*

# BUILDING YOUR BUSINESS THE Right-Brain Way

Also by Jennifer Lee

*The Right-Brain Business Plan*

# BUILDING YOUR BUSINESS THE
# Right-Brain Way

## SUSTAINABLE SUCCESS
## for the CREATIVE
## ENTREPRENEUR

# Jennifer Lee

**Illustrations by Kate Prentiss**

**Foreword by Michael Port**

New World Library
Novato, California

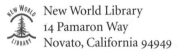 New World Library
14 Pamaron Way
Novato, California 94949

Illustrations by Kate Prentiss
Text design by Tona Pearce Myers

Library of Congress Cataloging-in-Publication Data is available.

First printing, April 2014
ISBN 978-1-60868-256-0
Printed in Canada on 100% postconsumer-waste recycled paper

 New World Library is proud to be a Gold Certified Environmentally Responsible Publisher. Publisher certification awarded by Green Press Initiative. www.greenpressinitiative.org

10  9  8  7  6  5  4  3  2  1

*For right-brain entrepreneurs around the world
who courageously take inspired actions
and make their big visions real, step by small step*

# Contents

# Foreword

I promise to keep this short, because I know you're here to absorb Jennifer Lee's brilliant new book, and I want you to get to it ASAP.

I use the word *absorb* rather than *read* intentionally. I could just as easily have gone with *consume*, *devour*, or, better yet, *relish*. Sure, Jennifer offers you the standard words-formed-info-sentences, but she also makes it easy for you to *see and deeply understand* what she's talking about through whimsical illustrations. As a result, you're able to truly internalize the ideas in this book — and there are many.

I'm not sure why it's taken so long for authors to realize how many people are visual learners and/or right-brain thinkers. Sometimes words just aren't enough. Fortunately for us, Jennifer is way ahead of the curve and knows that the two sides of the brain work best together. She provides both written and graphic ways to digest the material, so you can put your new insights into action immediately.

I love owning businesses. I love making money. I'm sure you do too. But much of the work we need to do to be successful in business is boring (and most business books, even more so). Writing out processes — boring. Writing proposals — really boring. Basic accounting — let's not even go there (at least, for 99.98 percent of all humanity). Again, it is our good fortune that Jennifer makes much of these necessary business practices fun, really fun, like that time I played a practical joke on the librarian, Mean Mrs. Manga (though I'll deny it 'til the day I die).

So, if you a own a spa, or do financial planning, or develop software, or run a large construction company, or tie elaborately shaped balloons for a living, and typically feel shut down when you read a business book, you'll be relieved to find a resource that speaks your right-brain language. You will love the visual play sheets. They'll spark your creativity as you map out key growth activities like improvements and innovations in your products and services, launch plans, and money-making methods.

Building a business is about a lot more than "following your passion," even though we right-brainers keep hoping otherwise. It's also about making sure you are productive and your business is profitable. The future belongs to the learner, not the learned; and the entrepreneur who learns in action leads the way. Fully absorbing *Building Your Business the Right-Brain Way* will give you the confidence to take risks, take action, and take control of your future.

Think big.

— Michael Port, *New York Times* bestselling author of
*Book Yourself Solid ILLUSTRATED*

# PART I

# THE LAY
# OF THE LAND

# 1 Your Creative Business Is a Work of Art

## Defining Your Own Success

Hello, my fellow right-brain entrepreneur!

When I created my first Right-Brain Business Plan, sitting at my kitchen table back in November 2007, I had no idea that that colorful and unusual approach would empower so many creative entrepreneurs around the world to launch their businesses in a way that made their hearts sing. It fills me with joy knowing that, as a result, more visionary souls, heart-centered professionals, and inspiring artists are out there making a positive difference through their work. Bravo, if you're one of those courageous creatives and have taken the leap to pursue your passions! I want to make sure you and your business are here to stay, so that you can keep on sharing your special gifts with the world.

That's where this book comes in. It picks up where *The Right-Brain Business Plan* book left off. While the earlier volume laid the foundation for clarifying your big vision, goals, and plan, *Building Your Business the*

*Right-Brain Way* takes you to the next steps, to growing your company by crafting how you offer your products or services, to engaging with more of your perfect customers, to diversifying and maximizing your moola-making methods, and more. You'll dive into doing the work and taking the actions needed to build a thriving and sustainable creative business. You'll learn to take your business more seriously, but in a way that still feels fun and manageable. Even if you've been in business for a while, the creative frameworks and visual tools in this book will spark fresh aha moments to help you move through blocks and get to your next level of success.

NOTE: Don't worry if you haven't read *The Right-Brain Business Plan* yet. As long as you have an overall sense of where your business is heading and the people you want to serve, you can build from that. Or if you've already created a Right-Brain Business Plan, I'll point out where you can reference your visual plan for supplemental insight. You can also check out the table on pages 213–14 to see which exercises from the previous book correspond to which chapters in this book.

## Business as Art: Trust Your Creative Process

As right-brainers we instinctively go through our own creative process any time we make something new. And as entrepreneurs we're creating new things in our businesses all the time. Yet somehow, when it comes to anything business related, we right-brainers presume we must follow an imposed left-brain, linear process. We dutifully struggle to fit ourselves into a set structure, and then we're either frustrated when things don't go as planned or disappointed when we find we're not as far along as we thought we "should" be.

Well, my right-brain friend, what if I told you that even in business, things are nonlinear and organic? Progress happens along a circuitous path of trying things out and seeing what sticks. Success unfolds over time, bit by bit. Yes, there are left-brain details that need to be handled along the way, but overall, business growth is actually more the result of right-brain genius than you may have thought. That's good news for us!

Your creative business is art. Consider how an intuitive painting takes shape. You begin by dabbing some paint here, adding a pop of color there. You follow your energy and listen to your gut as you fill in the canvas brushstroke by brushstroke. Maybe you started with an image in mind, but as forms and patterns appear you see the piece in new ways and the painting morphs into something you couldn't have predicted. An intuitive painting isn't produced pixel by pixel, line by line, in the sequential way that a predefined image is spit out of an ink-jet printer. And just like an intuitive painting, your creative business naturally emerges through play, discovery, and your refinement of each inspired action. Then, when one painting is done, you pick up your brush and start again, building your body of work.

In business we assume we go from point A to point B in a straight line. But really, it's more like the creative process you use in your craft, which may look a bit like this:

- You start from nothing.
- You find inspiration.
- You sketch, doodle, and brainstorm to flesh out the idea.
- You play with the idea, test it out, and explore it.
- You make it real by sharing it with the world.
- You discover and learn more about it as others interact with the idea.
- You reflect and refine the idea.
- You start again.

I bet you have big dreams about the difference you want to continue making in the world. That's why I want you to be successful and your business to stick around for the long term.

If you work yourself to the bone month after month only to barely make your numbers, that's not sustainable. If you push too hard and grow too fast without building a solid foundation, you might begin with a bang but eventually will hit a brick wall. You don't want to be a flash in the pan. You want to have staying power so you can continue to live your passion and share your gifts, right?

Sustainable businesses are scalable and resilient. Their owners constantly learn more about and refine their work by cycling through their creative process; they repeat their successes and increase their capacity to continue growing on their terms.

My business, just like yours, constantly evolves. When I began paying more attention to my company's overall health and having the right support and systems in place, my big vision and capacity for growth continued to expand.

## Success Your Way

The cool thing about owning your own business is that you get to call the shots and carve out your own definition of success.

Take a moment and ask yourself, "What does success look and feel like to me?" Is it about finding freedom and flexibility? Meeting certain monetary milestones? Making a meaningful impact? Receiving adoration and accolades? Fully expressing your creativity? Accomplishing lofty goals? Having fun? Conquering the world or changing lives one person at a time?

Be clear about what drives you. Don't succumb to external definitions of what success is supposed to look like. Rather, dig deep to uncover and honor what truly fulfills and serves you. It takes courage to claim your unique path to success.

### EXERCISE
### Sustainable Success Survey

The Sustainable Success Survey helps you check in on some of the key aspects of running your creative business that we cover in this book. In each section, answer the questions that are relevant to your business. At the end of each section of the survey you'll find a sliding scale between two key aspects. Mark a point on the scale to show where you are placing most of your attention. Depending on your priorities and your current situation, the point may be at either end of the spectrum or somewhere in the middle. There is no right or wrong score. The important takeaway is to recognize where you are on the scale. If you're not where you want to be, what can you do to shift your focus? Complete pertinent portions of this play sheet as often as you wish (weekly, monthly, or quarterly).

# SUSTAINABLE SUCCESS SURVEY

## Moola + MEANING

How much moola did you bring in this week?

How much moola did you spend this week?

What's your profit for the week?

Are you aligned with your values + vision?

Are you living your core message?

Are you making a positive impact big or small?

## Action + ease

What actions did you take this week to grow your business?

Have you made offers to potential clients this week?

Are your actions busywork or are they moola-making?

What's your energy level? Are you tired and worn out? Energized and raring to go? In your creative flow? Are you Steady Eddie?

What did you do this week to take care of yourself?

What can you let go of?

# Leadership + SUPPORT

Are you taking risks and stretching yourself?

How well are you cultivating existing relationships?

_____

How well are you building new relationships?

_____

How have you contributed to your own thought-leadership?

_____

Are you making informed decisions using left-brain data and by learning as you go?

_____
_____

Are you asking for help?

_____

Are you delegating work that is not in your genius zone?

_____

Are you developing and maintaining your Smooth Sailing Systems?

_____

Where do you need to focus your attention? _____
_____

What action do you need to do? By when? _____
_____

What are you celebrating? _____
_____

# SUSTAINABLE SUCCESS, IN THE WORDS OF FELLOW RIGHT-BRAIN ENTREPRENEURS

 "Success is happiness in all things and in all ways. Business success is waking up each day with a song in my heart, knowing that I am going to share my gifts with the world, live my true purpose and calling, and generally be happy and have lots of fun! Sustained business success is knowing I can do all that, receive moola for it, and feel my value and worth in the world."
— Bindi Shah

"I think success is living off of your vision and having a positive impact on other people. And a sustainable business is one that you can do forever."
— Mari Pfeiffer

"Sustainable means doable, easy, hassle-free."
— Patty Donahue

"Sustainable success is doing work that fulfills and inspires me and allows me the freedom to live a life overflowing with ease, adventure, laughter, and joy."
— Cynthia Patton

"Success = doing what you love, being with people you love, living on your own terms, expressing yourself freely, and earning the moola that helps you live the lifestyle that's right for you. Sustainable success = adapting your plans and expectations as you and the world around you change, without sacrificing any of the above."
— Mary Maru Wright

"Sustainable success means the business is vital — is life giving. It is a business that continues to grow with the least effort. It also means the business is life affirming and it positively impacts the people who work in the space."
— Mary K. Clark

"Success means having quality, deep, rich relationships — because in the end, you can have all the fame and fortune you desire, but if you don't have true friends, you've really missed out. Sustained success means creating the kind of lifestyle that allows for the ebb and flow of business and life while still providing for my needs and growth."
— Tammi Spruill

# How to Use This Book

Let this book be your go-to guide for building your sustainable business the right-brain way. You can approach the book chapter by chapter, or feel free to dip into the parts or sections you know you need to address first or explore further. The key is to take action in the real world, because that's where the true magic happens.

The book is divided into four parts:

*Part I. The Lay of the Land.* This chapter and chapter 2 help you get the lay of the land through some initial assessments of where your business is now. You'll get a sense of your business's current health, and you can build from there.

*Part II. Setting the Stage for Yourself and Your Right Peeps.* Start here if you need to clarify your core message (chapter 3), build your platform, or engage more with your tribe to learn how to best meet their needs (chapter 4).

*Part III. Getting Down to Business.* Dive into this section if you already know who your perfect customers are and you've developed strong relationships with them. You're ready to get down to business, launch your products and services (chapters 5 and 6), and make more moola (chapter 7). Even if you already have products or services, or both, in place, this section will help you expand by diversifying and leveraging your moola-making methods.

*Part IV. Sustaining Your Success.* The final part of the book guides you through getting the support and systems in place so your business runs smoothly (chapters 8 and 9). We end by embracing ease, which may be the most important lesson of all when it comes to sustainable success. Visit chapter 10 whenever you're feeling stuck or depleted and need a pick-me-up.

Throughout this book you'll find the following headings and icons:

 *Right-Brain Reflections.* Occasionally you'll be prompted with a question to help deepen your awareness or understanding of a thought pattern, situation, or intention. Your answers may come through journaling, drawing, or having a conversation with one of your creative cohorts.

 *Illustrated Play Sheets.* Writing your thoughts down on paper is one of the best ways to start making them real. The images and metaphors used in these fun and colorful play sheets will engage your creativity and intuition, helping you to gain new insights into your business. You can also download PDF versions at www.rightbrainbusinessplan .com/rbbiz.

 *Exercises.* You'll find creative exercises in most chapters. These may include intuitive explorations, artistic assignments, or experiential activities. While these short projects are meant to spark insights and help provide clarity, by no means do you need to complete all of them. Just choose the ones that will help you work through places where you've been stuck or that you know need more attention. And by the way, you don't need any special artistic skills or talent to do the visual or creative assignments. Just have fun!

 *Right-Brain Entrepreneur Spotlights.* Throughout this book you'll get to meet creative business owners just like you who have demonstrated the use of their right-brain genius. I hope their journeys inspire you to take risks and keep moving forward. Some have had their businesses for several years and have used their right-brain abilities to reinvent themselves, grow the online part of their businesses, expand their teams, or diversify their moola-making methods. Others are still in the first few years of business, so they're laying foundations for sustainable businesses.

 *Left-Brain Chill Pills and Right-Brain Boosters.* Since these quick tips were such a hit in the previous book, you're getting a refill prescription here. Right-Brain Boosters are bits of inspiration to enhance your creative intuition, and Left-Brain Chill Pills are short suggestions to quiet your judging mind. Take doses of each as needed (doctor's orders!).

*Tips.* Once in a while, I'll point out something to watch out for or make note of.

*Action Accelerators.* As you'll see, one of the guiding principles in this book is to take action. So, in each chapter I'll urge you to take at least one suggested small action out in the real world. Remember each small action gets you closer to your big vision.

*Left-Brain Checklists.* Each chapter wraps up with a handy-dandy checklist to help ensure that you've covered all the important pieces. Of course, not all items are mandatory, so feel free to skip the ones that don't apply to you. The checklist police are not going to fine you if not all the boxes are ticked.

Cass Mullane, founder of Prosper Creatively, fully embraces the idea that her creative business is a work of art, as seen in this quirky and fun self-portrait she quilted as part of her Right-Brain Business Plan.

# MEET MR. SKETCH,
## YOUR BROAD-STROKE BUSINESS BUDDY

It's probably no big surprise that I'm a fan of colorful markers. I went through a phase when I always had my set of Staedtler fine-tipped pens with me so I could carefully write down precise (and of course pretty) notes.

One day while talking to my mentor, Andrea J. Lee, I shared with her how overwhelmed I was as I geared up for my first-ever video summit to help launch my first book. My head was spinning with details, what-ifs, and labor-intensive logistics.

Andrea simply said to me, "Jenn, six-figure business owners use Mr. Sketch."

What she meant was: rather than fixating on the minutiae and painstakingly planning while using my Staedtler fine-tipped pen, I could, metaphorically, cover the same ground more effectively and efficiently with the broad strokes of a Mr. Sketch marker. That's the type of strategic shift that takes creative entrepreneurs to their next level of success.

Try it now:

**BOX 1**

Use a fine-tipped marker or ballpoint pen to color in this blank box, being careful not to leave any white space showing.

**BOX 2**

Now get your wide-tipped marker, Mr. Sketch, or thick felt-tipped pen and color in this blank box, being careful not to leave any white space showing.

My guess is that Box 1 took a heck of a lot longer to color in, line by fine line, whereas you probably filled in Box 2 with a single broad stroke of your Mr. Sketch.

Likewise, don't fret about the itty-bitty details when a simpler solution will yield an even better result.

As you make your way through this book, there are some key things that I want you to keep in mind.

*Be uniquely you and embrace your creativity.* This book is not about giving you a cookie-cutter, step-by-step solution. You are a creative person, after all, and your business is just as creative as you are. Examples and spotlights are provided, but they are by no means blueprints to follow. Building your business the right-brain way is making it your own and making it work for you. Add your own touch of right-brain genius.

*Dream big but start small.* Don't get seduced by the bigness of your big vision and expect to achieve it all at once. Your big vision will unfold over time, bit by bit, so break things down into manageable pieces and go from there.

*Keep it simple.* Opt for easy, broad strokes instead of fine-lined, complicated solutions.

*Take action, make it real, and tweak as you go.* Many of the exercises will emphasize turning your thoughts into something tangible that you can share, test, and tweak sooner rather than later. People can't buy a brilliant idea that's locked away in your head. Be willing to take action and put yourself out there, even when you don't feel ready and even if your idea is not yet perfect. You'll actually learn more and gain more clarity the more you interact with your idea and get feedback.

*Look for the learning and repeat what works.* Always have your eyes peeled for valuable new insights to help you continuously improve. Then, when you find something that works, keep doing it until it doesn't work anymore.

*Consider where you are headed* and *don't get ahead of yourself.* Stay ahead of the curve but don't advance so fast that you overwhelm yourself. Make sure you have a solid foundation first to support your future vision.

*Recognize where you've come from.* Even as you move forward, also acknowledge how far you've come, each step of the way. Recognizing past achievements and reflecting on your success helps keep your circuitous progress in perspective.

*Know thyself.* Building a business is a journey accompanied by personal growth. Understand what makes you tick, and be willing to courageously move past your edges. When you transform yourself, you transform your business.

Throughout this book, you'll engage both sides of your brain. Your right brain will help you tap into your creativity and intuition. Your left brain will help you arrange the details and structure that will enable you to take action in the real world.

## Let's Get Going!

The best way to grow your business is to go out there, share your useful and valuable gifts with your right people, and get paid for it. Now, I know this is sometimes easier said than done, which is why in the following pages I share with you some proven creative strategies for making your dreams real. So, let's get going!

# Tending Your Entrepreneurial Ecosystem

## Is Your Business Blooming and Booming?

When I first started my business in 2003, I didn't truly acknowledge that I was indeed in business. I was just a creative person who liked to coach people and who liked to make art. I was simply following my passions and helping people. I didn't think of myself as an entrepreneur, especially since I was doing all of that on the side while I continued to climb the corporate ladder. But when I finally took the leap from my day job in 2006, I knew I had to start taking my business more seriously. I gradually moved from just working with individual clients, to running groups and courses, to creating products, to writing an award-winning and bestselling book, to licensing my programs, and more. And lo and behold, over the years my one-person operation grew into an expanding enterprise that now includes a small support team and more than seventy licensed facilitators around the world. Of course, as we talked about in chapter 1, the actual journey hasn't been so linear. It's been full of twists and turns, and ups and downs, in the creative process. Now that I've been in business for more than a decade, I've seen my business mature into a system that needs to be consciously tended to and cared for in order to continue thriving.

Your creative business, too, is a living and breathing entity, and it needs TLC to blossom and prosper. Whether you're fairly new to your business, or you've been at your work for a while, it's helpful to take a step back and check in — to assess the overall health of your Entrepreneurial Ecosystem, especially if you want sustained success. So before we dive into the rest of the book, let's take a look at where your business is right now and identify what's needed for your business to fully bloom.

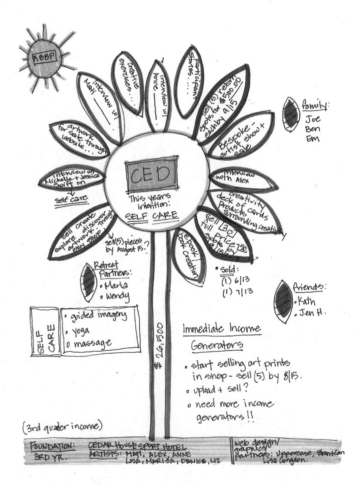

Sarah Stevenson, owner of Redlinedesign, created this Entrepreneurial Ecosystem to specifically assess the retreat aspect of her business.

For this exercise we'll use the fun visual metaphor of a flower — which you'll turn into a doodle — to help you assess some of the key pieces that go into your business success. Make sure to keep your doodle handy, since we'll come back to this assessment throughout the book.

What you'll need:

- A large blank piece of paper
- Colorful markers, crayons, or pencils

Scan to watch the video.

You can also refer to the Entrepreneurial Ecosystem play sheet on page 22; however, lots of right-brain entrepreneurs have enjoyed the self-expression of drawing their own doodles.

To walk through this exercise with me in a short video clip, scan the QR code with your smartphone.

### Big Vision

Your business probably stems from something you're really excited about bringing into the world. And I imagine that, as a creative entrepreneur, you have a big vision of where you want to take your business. In the top right-hand corner of the paper, jot down a few notes about the big vision of your business. This is the limitless, blue-sky thinking that right-brainers are known for. Let yourself dream big.

Where do you see yourself and your business heading? What does success look like to you?

If you'd like to add some images, include a few collage elements in the

## SOME THINGS TO KEEP IN MIND

Just a few notes on the creative exercises: These are not about making beautiful art or about having masterpieces. These creative exercises are meant to spark your intuition and help you visually express your ideas on paper. So have fun and get messy! No artistic skill or talent is required; tell your inner critic to take a hike. And please, no wordsmithing here either. It's more about getting something down on paper to work from. The real value of this exercise (and others like it in the book) is seeing how all the pieces fit together; don't get hung up on getting each section right or on making it look good. (Sustained-success hint: letting go of being "right" or making things look "good" is also a good practice at the macro-business level, so think of this as great training.)

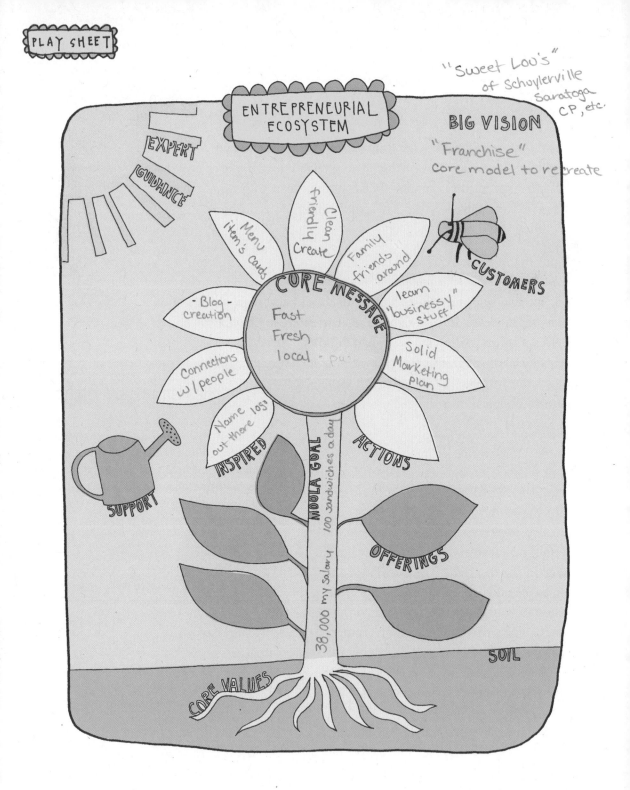

background. But don't go overboard, because you'll be drawing other elements on most of the paper.

## Core Message

Now, draw a circle in the top center of the paper. This is the center of your flower. Inside the circle, write a brief description of what you're taking a stand for in your business. This is the core message that your business is based on. Think of it as the irresistible nectar that attracts your honeybees (a.k.a. your right people).

**TIP**

If you went through *The Right-Brain Business Plan* book, feel free to reflect back on the Big Vision Visualization and Big Vision Collage exercises. If you haven't done the Big Vision Visualization and want some entirely optional extra guidance in connecting with your big dreams for your business, you can download and listen to the MP3 by visiting www.rightbrainbusinessplan.com/rbbiz.

Don't worry if you're not able to fully articulate your core message yet; we'll cover this in greater depth in the next chapter. So for now, just to get you started, here are a few prompts to help you fill in the center of your flower.

- What are you taking a stand for in your business? fresh
- What impact do you want to make with your work? fast
- What are you passionate about, and how are you helping people? local

## Inspired Actions

Next draw some petals around the center of your flower. In each of the petals write one of the actions you're taking to move closer to your big vision. For this particular exercise, your list of actions doesn't need to be exhaustive or superdetailed. Just highlight either the main activities you focus your time and energy on in your business, or the key tasks of the current projects you're working on. I call them inspired actions because you want the activities to be aligned with your values and big vision, not simply things you think you "should" be doing.

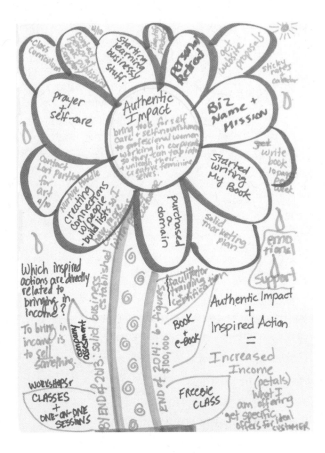

The Entrepreneurial Ecosystem assessment showed Helene Rose, founder of Be Brilliant Network, that her inspired actions need to be directly related to income generation in order to hit her moola goal.

## Moola Goal

Now get your green marker and draw two vertical lines to make the stem of your flower. Inside the stem, write in your overall moola goal for the year. This is the gross income you want to make before expenses.

We'll go into moola-making in more depth throughout this book. Right now we're simply doing an initial pass to get some numbers on paper, so don't stress about it. Just use your gut instinct, and know that you can always come back and revise this later.

Once you have your number, you can shade in the stem like a fundraising thermometer to represent how much money you've brought in to date. For example, if your goal is to make $100,000, and you've already made $25,000, you can shade the bottom quarter of your stem to make a nice visual gauge of earnings to date.

Look at the number you wrote in your stem. Does it feel doable and like you're on track? Or does it feel a bit out of reach? Are you clear about what you need to do to make that amount of money?

This section of the Ecosystem, the moola stem of the flower, is typically where right-brain entrepreneurs may see a disconnect between their financial goals and what their bank statements say. Before you get discouraged, there are a couple of places we can make some simple adjustments that can make a big difference.

First, take a look at your inspired-action petals and ask yourself: Are your current actions bringing you closer to hitting your moola goal? Or are they distractions or busywork that keep you from the heart of your business?

At this point in the assessment, most of the right-brain entrepreneurs I work with can identify at least a few ways they can adjust their to-do list to focus on more profitable actions. For instance, rather than having petals about printing up business cards, researching which headset to use for the live video class they've been dreaming up, and obsessing over unnecessary updates to their website, they choose more profitable petals. They may concentrate on following up with potential clients who have expressed interest in their work, reaching out to galleries to show their art, or having a sale on one of their products to bring in cash now.

Second, we'll look at the next portion of the flower, which is a big part of bridging the gap between your moola goal and the money coming in.

## What You Offer

At this point you have the basic elements of your flower, including the center of the flower (your core message), the petals (the actions you're taking to support the Big Vision), and the stem (your moola goal for the year).

Next, you're going to draw leaves on your stem. For every product or service you offer, draw a leaf and write in a description of it and the estimated income you can earn from it. For example, an artist might have a leaf for her commissioned paintings ($3,000 each, five pieces per year, which equals $15,000), a leaf for prints sold on Etsy ($10,000 total sales per year), a leaf for original artwork sold at galleries ($2,000 each, five pieces per year, which equals $10,000), and a leaf for the painting retreats she offers ($3,000 per retreat, four retreats per year, which equals $12,000). The total of $47,000 comes close to the artist's moola goal of $50,000 for the year. Now she can either think of an additional leaf or two to earn another $3,000 or figure out ways to increase the amount on an existing leaf — like, let's say, running a fifth retreat).

You can put existing products or services on the left side of the stem and planned ones on the right side. Don't worry if you're struggling with filling out the leaves or you're having trouble adding enough leaves to equal your moola goal. We'll address this in more detail in chapter 5, where we look at packaging your gifts and crafting what you offer. We'll also discuss it in chapter 7, where we talk about the fastest path to cash (you may even want to skip ahead and dive into that one right now).

For another example, here's a peek at the flower of designer Mary Maru Wright. Her company, Mary Maru Design, has two main service categories, web design and print design, so she created two large leaves. Mary explains,

Within each service category leaf, I list a half dozen or more services along with minimum prices. For example, in the web design leaf I added custom HTML email design, WordPress micro sites, web maintenance, and so on. For the print design leaf, I've listed brochures, trade show booth graphics, logo and identity packages, ads, and so on. I like having the two big leaves rather than a dozen or more smaller ones, because it keeps the flower uncluttered and easier for me to see at a glance.

Seeing my service offerings with prices in the context of the flower model has helped me see that I need to continue cultivating long-term client relationships with customers who prefer to work with one designer for all their marketing needs. For a quarterly goal of, say, $15,000, that means I need to have about three clients who each plan to spend $5,000 in whatever mix of services — preferably one bigger item in the range of $2,500–$3,000 or more, plus smaller items throughout the year that can be done easily in between.

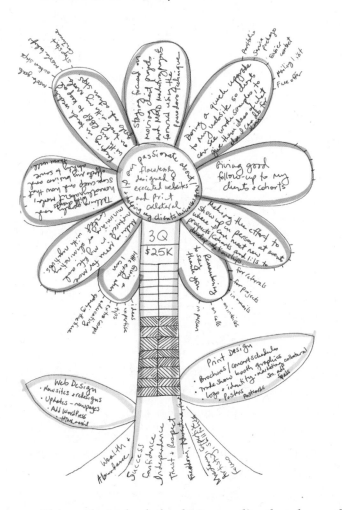

The Entrepreneurial Ecosystem assessment helped designer Mary Maru Wright realize that focusing on longer-term client relationships will help her maximize her moola-making.

This analysis also helped Mary realize that she can let go of some of her previous smaller offers that are not sustainable. She told me, "With a per client goal of about $5,000, it also becomes clear that it doesn't make sense for me, as a one-person shop, to offer a $200 postcard design to a client whose only order for the year is that one item."

The big vision of writing coach Jackie Blain is to empower writers and give people access to their writer selves. Once she realized this was her focus, she was able to put aside some leaves she was working on — including an e-book that she decided to turn into a free offer in order to build her list — which helped her save time and energy. And she was able to give herself permission to trim away old leaves related to tutoring ESL students and doing SAT prep, because they didn't fit in with her flower and overall Ecosystem.

Do the leaves add up to the moola goal on your stem? If not, what adjustments can you make to what you're offering? Are there leaves you can trim off that are not serving you?

It's one thing to have a stated moola goal, and it's another to make sure that the actions you're taking are profit-generating ones (not just busywork) AND that you're offering services or products (leaves on your flower stem) that add up to the moola goal on your stem. If they don't add up, you'll always have a gap between what you want to earn and what you're actually making.

Take a deep breath. You've done a lot so far....

Okay, now that you have the body of your flower drawn, let's get to some of the other parts of the Entrepreneurial Ecosystem.

## The Sun

In the top left-hand corner of your paper, draw a sun. The sun represents expert guidance and support. Its radiant beams shine light on new opportunities or potential blind spots. Inside the sun, write the names of the luminaries you surround yourself with. These can include your mentors, teachers, and role models, as well as trusted advisors who provide you with their expert guidance.

If your sun is blank, begin building relationships with mentors who can show you the ropes, or start working with teachers whose message resonates with you. Successful entrepreneurs have access to experienced professionals in their circle who help them identify areas of growth, and who can illuminate a path through the dark patches. Sure, you may be able to figure these issues out on your own, but most likely it would take more time and effort to fumble through them alone than to figure them out while standing on the shoulders of giants.

## The Soil

Near the bottom of your doodle, make sure you include some soil. The soil provides much-needed nutrients to your flower. The soil is enriched with the information, knowledge, and resources needed to grow your business. Do you have the skills required to take your business to the next level? Are you familiar with the trends affecting your industry or your clients? Do you have access to data to help you make educated decisions? If not, how can you fortify your foundation with valuable and helpful information and resources? You don't need to overload yourself. Instead, find the right amount of information to keep the nutrients in the soil in balance.

One surprise ingredient that makes for nutrient-rich soil is, in fact, fertilizer. You know how crappy you feel when you've made a mistake and things don't go the way you planned? Well, guess what? That "crap" actually enriches the soil with learning and experience, so be willing to take risks, make mistakes, and learn from them to continue growing.

Lou Shackleton and her cohorts at the You Can Hub articulated the core values that inspire their nonprofit organization's work in the community.

## The Roots

Draw some roots from the flower stem into the earth. The roots represent your core values. Your values are what provide meaning to your work and are what your business is grounded in. These are the things that are most important to you and that you can't live without. One helpful way of identifying your core values is to think back on times in your life when you felt fully alive. Describe those peak moments, and then choose the key words that represent what lights you up. Another way to articulate your core values is to look at what makes you angry. This can be an indicator that one of your core values is being dishonored.

On each root, write a core value or related string of core values. For instance, one string might be: "creativity/self-expression/uniqueness." And another might be: "adventure/risk/courage."

How are these values showing up in your business (and your life)? Are you making decisions based on your core values or based on external "shoulds"? When your business is deeply rooted by your core values, it can withstand even the harshest storms. If your core values are not strongly represented in your business, these fragile roots will make it difficult for your business to stay grounded and be resilient during challenging times.

## The Watering Can

Next, draw a watering can (and please, remember this isn't about being artistic!). The watering can symbolizes the emotional support that helps keep your flower strong and vibrant. We all know what happens when a flower doesn't get enough water, right? It shrivels up. Have there been times since you started your business when you've felt alone and you wilted under pressure? I know I've been there, and I see it happen to other creative entrepreneurs, too. We're so busy trying to push through on our own that we forget how important it is to have lifelines to help us get through hard times. Besides, think of how life affirming it can be to have wonderful friends and colleagues who also celebrate with us and help us thrive.

On the watering can, write the names of the people in your life who provide you with emotional support. This support could be in the form of encouragement, a shoulder to cry on, an empathetic ear. These people are the first ones you call when you have some good news to announce, your nurture huddle (a group of supportive cohorts), and other people you can turn to for trusted feedback who are willing to tell you the hard truth. If your watering can is running low, make time to cultivate connections with kindred spirits and develop these important friendships.

## The Honeybees

Remember what you wrote in your core message in the middle of the flower? That core message is the nectar that attracts your honeybees. The honeybees are the fans and customers who are drawn to your work and who help to spread the word about you by carrying your message. Do you have a sense of who the honeybees are that you attract?

Are you attracting a whole swarm of your right peeps or just a few influential ones who can help put you on the map? Are you getting the kind of engagement you want?

We'll cover attracting your right peeps in chapter 4.

Feel free to draw in any other elements that make up your Entrepreneurial Ecosystem.

## Assess Your Entrepreneurial Ecosystem

Now take a step back from your Entrepreneurial Ecosystem sketch and reflect on the following questions.

Are you clear about what goes in the center of your Business Flower? Why you are doing what you're doing? If you're not certain, pay special attention to the next chapter, about articulating your core message.

Do you have empty petals on your flower? That means you probably need to take additional concrete, doable, and value-added actions to help you move forward. If you're not sure what actions to take, at the end of each chapter you can refer to the left-brain checklist for ideas. Make sure, though, that the actions are aligned with your big vision, and that they are related to making moola in some form.

If you notice that you're missing leaves on your stem, and you're not sure how to reach the moola goal on your stem, start brainstorming about some leaves you can add to fill the gaps and increase your moola-making ability. In chapter 5 we will cover crafting the way you offer your products or services, but it's helpful to start thinking about this now, even at a high level.

Lacking enough water, sunshine, or soil to support your flower's growth? The final chapter will show you some strategies for sustaining your success, including ways to get the support you need in order to thrive. These are the ongoing practices that will help you tend the garden of your Entrepreneurial Ecosystem.

Even if your flower needs more petals, leaves, sun, or water, the cool thing is that now you have a sense of what to tend to in your Entrepreneurial Ecosystem so that you can create sustainable success for your business. And it's good to check once in a while to see if weeds are choking off your flower. What unwanted extras are getting in the way of your growth?

Remember to keep your Business Flower handy as you go through the rest of this book. We'll cover all the different pieces in the following chapters to make sure your creative business is not only blooming but also booming.

# PART II

# SETTING THE STAGE FOR YOURSELF AND YOUR RIGHT PEEPS

# Taking a Stand and Making an Impact

## What's Your Core Message?

Right-brain entrepreneur that you are, you no doubt birthed your business out of something you're innately passionate about. Your creative work is an authentic expression of who you are and what you stand for. You love what you do. Sometimes, though, you can be so close to your craft that articulating the heart of your work can be surprisingly challenging, right? You live and breathe your essence. Your way of working and being comes so naturally to you that it can be hard to put into words what you instinctively know and offer, let alone try to package it up and sell it to someone who will find it valuable.

Yet when you can clearly communicate your core message through compelling content, interactions, and experiences, your right peeps can't help but be drawn to you. Your work resonates with your perfect customers because you're speaking their language. You *get* them. They see a part of themselves in you and what you offer. So the good news is:

the more you can be fully and authentically you, the more your right peeps will gravitate to you. Yay! What a relief, right?

When you share your core message, it's like a beacon that helps you stand out from the crowd and guides your right people to you. But they won't know how to find you unless you're talking about what matters to you. So, let's help you own and share your core message.

As we dive into the rest of this chapter, it's a great time to refer back to what you wrote in the center of your Business Flower in chapter 2's Entrepreneurial Ecosystem exercise. Even if you noted only a few words about your core message there, it's the start of cultivating the compelling nectar that your perfect customers will be irresistibly drawn to.

The exercises in this chapter will help you articulate what it is you stand for. These creative activities are meant to spark your own intuitive process as you explore your core message and the impact you make through your products and services. Keep in mind that your business can have an overall core message that your products and services align with, and that each of your products and services may in turn have even more specific messages that speak of the unique benefits they provide. The insights you uncover here will help support your work in future chapters as you craft your product and service offers and lovingly launch them into the world.

In this chapter you'll also meet other right-brain entrepreneurs, who will prove that each creative soul's message can be unique. They'll inspire you to courageously embrace your calling. You'll see that core messages evolve over time. Don't expect to have it all figured out from the get-go. In fact, by sharing your message and engaging with your people, you'll refine what you stand for and discover what resonates with you and your perfect customers.

This bright and colorful mixed-media piece by Sarah Stevenson of Redlinedesign represents her core message, "Surprise Yourself. Through her creative work and retreats, she inspires people to take a leap and do something unexpected and fun.

To help you get your creative juices flowing, especially if you're not exactly sure you can articulate your message, here are a few journaling prompts. See if any of these spark some ideas for you.

- What are you taking a stand for?
- Name something that upsets or frustrates you.
- What do you wish people knew? I mean really, really got in their bones and deep in their soul.
- If you could bottle up a magic potion that would changed people's lives for the better, what exactly would that potion do? What would it be called?

Magic Potion

TIP

If you went through the *Right-Brain Business Plan* book, feel free to have any of the following pieces handy in case they provide supplemental clues that help with the core-message exercises. The ones marked with an asterisk may be especially useful:

Big-Vision Collage
Values cards
Passion and Purpose Proclamation*
Business Self-Portrait*
Business Landscape

And of course, if you haven't done any of those optional exercises, don't worry. Just focus on the main activities here.

- Name something missing from the world that would make it better.

When you're done journaling your responses, what themes, if any, do you notice? What jumps out at you? Remember, this doesn't have to be the all-encompassing big message. In fact, over the course of your business's growth your message may evolve.

## Uncover and Articulate Your Core Message

To help you uncover or more clearly articulate your core message, this chapter offers three exercises. Use whichever one speaks to you, or do more than one. And remember, there's no right or wrong way to play with these creative exercises. Simply let them tap into what your right-brain genius already knows.

### EXERCISE
### Design Your Fantastical Freeway Billboard

In *L.A. Story*, one of my favorite movies, a magical freeway sign lights up with special announcements that seem to speak directly to Steve Martin's character, the wacky weatherman Harris K. Telemacher. Throughout the movie this chatty billboard's quirky communiqués shift Harris's once-jaded perspectives and embolden him to take more risks, ultimately helping him find more meaning and love in his life.

Imagine that you had your own fantastical freeway sign that let you communicate life-changing messages to your right people. While the sign in *L.A. Story* was able to flash only a limited number of characters, these days some fancy freeway billboards are actually giant full-color video

FANTASTICAL FREEWAY

billboard

## RIGHT-BRAIN BOOSTER

Play with others. If you're drawing a blank with these core-message exercises, it may be helpful to seek an outside perspective. Invite past clients to share how your work has influenced them. Ask your creative cohorts and trusted colleagues: "If you were to imagine a billboard for my product or service, what would be on it?" Have them send you some words or pictures to include in your collage.

screens, so let your creativity run wild as you think about what you could display. What images, metaphors, symbols, colors, or words would convey your message? If there were a tagline, what would it say? What impact would your billboard have? Whom would you want your message to reach? How would your sign change their lives?

Use the Fantastical Freeway Billboard illustrated play sheet to sketch out or collage a billboard bearing your core message.

What you'll need:

- A plain piece of paper or the Fantastical Freeway Billboard illustrated play sheet
- Markers
- Magazines (optional)
- Glue stick (optional)
- Scissors (optional)

Remember your billboard doesn't need to fully make sense, and it certainly doesn't need to be perfect. This is just a starting place for you to express yourself using your right-brain intuition.

After you create your Fantastical Freeway Billboard, jot down a few notes. Simply notice what feels important to you.

### EXERCISE
### What Would You Tattoo across Your Chest?

Taking the freeway sign concept one step further, let me introduce you to Laura Burns, founder of Laura Burns Consulting and a licensed Right-Brain Business Plan facilitator from Texas. Laura is actually her

# RIGHT-BRAIN ENTREPRENEUR SPOTLIGHT

Photographer and e-course leader Vivienne McMaster embodies her "Be Your Own Beloved" core message in her business. Vivienne says,

The core message of my work with Be Your Own Beloved is that you are worthy of self-love here and now, and that self-portraiture can be a powerful tool for use on your path to self-compassion. It actually took me a few years to really become clear about my core message. I had been teaching self-portrait photography classes for a while, but with a focus on artistry, storytelling, and learning about the camera. The "Be Your Own Beloved" message was always at the core of why I made self-portraits, and I wove it into my classes. But it took me a while to realize that there were so many people for whom that particular message resonated. Once I owned my purpose, I realized that everything needed to align with that core message, be it a collaboration, a new class, an e-book, or any other offering. Otherwise I'd let it go.

Vivienne expresses her "Be Your Own Beloved" core message through self-portraiture like this fun image, which reminds us to love ourselves.

own walking billboard. She is so committed to her core message, "Married to Amazement," that in 2010 she literally had it tattooed across her chest.

That quote, from Mary Oliver's poem "When Death Comes," inspires Laura to live life by doing the things that are most important to her and to make every moment count. Laura says, "The tattoo is a daily reminder to take chances and put myself out there. Sometimes I succeed and sometimes I fail, but at least I've embraced the opportunity and can learn and grow from each experience."

What would you tattoo across your chest? Laura Burns's boldly emblazoned body art helps keep her mission and purpose close to heart.

When people notice her bold body art, they often stop to ask her what it means. Being the great coach that she is, Laura lives her mission by asking, "What does it mean to you?" Inevitably this leads to amazing conversations and connections. She says she loves how her tattoo brings her right people out of the woodwork.

Not only does her core message influence how she lives her life, but it also inspires the products and services she offers. In her coaching and her latest interactive workbook, she helps people transition from soul-crushing careers to starting their own amazing businesses that they love.

What would you tattoo across your chest? Now, of course you don't have to get permanently inked to make a statement. Try your message on for size by writing it in marker across your chest or on your arm or any other symbolic place on your body. For example, if your message is about embracing your creativity, scribble it on your hands. Or if it's about spending more time outdoors, write it on your bare feet.

As you physically wear your words, notice what it feels like to embody your message. Do you stand a little taller? What emotions are you sensing? What's your energy like when you allow yourself to be in the skin of your statement?

# RIGHT-BRAIN ENTREPRENEUR SPOTLIGHT

Graphic designer Mary Maru Wright illustrates how these core-message exercises can help you articulate what you're taking a stand for, and how that can translate into the way you offer your product or service.

Three things frustrate me: (1) ineffective and unattractive marketing materials and websites; (2) marketing materials and websites with too many bells and whistles, too many design embellishments, and too much copy; and (3) clients who begin the conversation with: "There's really no budget, but we'd like to..."

I wish more business owners knew that first impressions count. And since websites and other marketing pieces are often what a customer sees before meeting the business reps—if they ever meet at all—making a credible and professional first impression through these means is critical.

I'm taking a stand for design that is effective, attractive, uncluttered, and yes, sometimes expensive, but always of high value.

For a billboard in Times Square, my core message might say: "Take a look around. This is what you don't want your marketing materials to look like. Unless your business is in Times Square."

How all this informs my offer: First, I have an informational PDF in the works called "How to Plan for Your Business Website," which I'm hoping will instruct business owners and marketers in how to pull together their materials for their websites so they can work efficiently with a web designer. And second, other possible informational PDFs could be: "Decluttering Your Marketing Materials," "Marketing Design Dos and Don'ts," and "Marketing Design Crimes."

I've realized after working through this exercise that there's a disconnect between the things I mention here and the messages I'm sharing with the world. I'd love to get to the point where there's more synergy between my thoughts and my actions.

Feeling extra brave? Walk around outside with your temporary tattoo in view and strike up conversations with people who may notice your message. Who do you attract? What do you learn from engaging with those who are curious about your message or who tell you it resonates with them?

Journal what you discover, and take a photo of your body art to remind you of what it feels like to share your message with the world.

## Why Is It Important to Have a Core Message?

Most likely there are other fabulous folks out there who are working in the same field as you. Earlier you met Vivienne McMaster, a photographer and e-course leader. There are other photographers who are e-course leaders, too, but Vivienne's "Be Your Own Beloved" message helps her stand out. And as she stated, her core message helps her decide what opportunities to say yes to. Not only is it a guiding light that enables your perfect customers to find you, but it's also your own guiding light that helps you focus on what to offer.

### EXERCISE
### Pen Secret Love Notes

Perhaps flashy billboard signs or permanent body art isn't your cup of tea. For a more low-key approach, consider writing secret love notes to your perfect customers and tucking them in public places around where you live or where your community congregates, like at bookstores, coffee shops, or art stores.

What would your message say? Who would you want to receive these love notes? How would you want the message to affect these individuals? How would your people be different after reading your wonderful, heartfelt words? Even if you don't actually leave them lying around for people to find, write one to practice getting your message on paper.

## RIGHT-BRAIN ENTREPRENEUR SPOTLIGHT

 A 2011 trip to Bali inspired Melissa Gazzaneo's business and core message. She went there to visit her mom, who was teaching organic gardening at a small school. Melissa's mom had encouraged her to pack some art supplies for the kids, since the school had none. So Melissa arrived with a suitcase full of creative goodies and for a few weeks taught the kids English through art.

Melissa says, "The kids in the class loved it, and many more began showing up, knowing there would be something fun in store for them. During my time there, I realized I wanted to somehow bring art supplies to kids around the world, but I was not sure how to make that happen."

Fast-forward a year: Melissa founded her company, Reskü, on the core message "Repurposed for a Purpose." The company sells hip, urban bags, and while there are plenty of handmade messenger bags and iPad cases out there, Reskü's core message helps Melissa's products stand out. The bags are made from recycled firefighter gear, so they're durable and water resistant. And part of the proceeds from each bag goes to local and global organizations supporting the arts for children.

Reskü has already donated art supplies to the East Oakland Boxing Association and made its first delivery of art supplies to a school in a small village near Munduk, high in the mountains of Bali. Melissa says, "If those art supplies help a child learn a language, express his feelings, get through some kind of trauma, or develop into an artist himself, all the effort is totally worth it."

# RIGHT-BRAIN ENTREPRENEUR SPOTLIGHT

Your core message may come to you when you least expect it. For coach Amy Christensen of Expand Outdoors, her core message, "Embrace Your Inner Badass," emerged on a particularly challenging rock climb when she joked to a friend that she really needed her inner badass to come out and play.

Amy describes her inner badass as "the part of me who lives unapologetically—with passion and gusto. She faces her fears, acknowledges them, and still leaps into life's challenges and joys. She is part of me who is sassy, fun, and a little impish."

On the mountain, Amy's motto helped her complete that demanding climb. Off the mountain, her motto started to take on a life of its own as she realized that it resonated with lots of other women too. Now her offerings target women who want to reclaim their courage and push past their comfort zones.

Pay attention to those moments in your life when something resonates and really sticks. That's a clue to what could be your core message.

This mixed-media piece created by Amy Christensen represents the values and core message of her business, Expand Outdoors. She included elements from nature, such as rocks and leaves, to represent her connection to the earth and outdoors.

Now that you've explored your core message, circle back to your Business Flower from chapter 2 and, if you'd like, update or refine what you put in the center of your flower, based on what you learned from these exercises. Remember, it doesn't have to be perfectly phrased. The idea is to capture your thoughts so that you can practice sharing your message.

### Say It Loud and Say It Proud

The more you give voice to your message, the more comfortable you will get with it — and the more feedback you'll get about what resonates with the peeps you want to attract. You won't know if your message is making an impact if you don't share it with others and see how it lands.

## RIGHT-BRAIN BOOSTER

You are an expert in your own ideas and experience. Remember, you are unique. You have your special blend of background, passions, talents, and ideas that only you bring together, and that no one else can share in the way that you can. The more you can bring your full, authentic self into your work, the more you will attract your right people.

Tammi Spruill, founder of Fruition, recognized that many creatives resist branding because they feel it will put them in a box. She used that challenge as an inspiration for developing her BRANDvolution core message and approach. Her signature BRANDvolution Board here depicts the experience of freedom and empowerment she wants to create for her clients.

How does your message stack up against how you're showing up in the world right now? Does what you're currently communicating align with your core message? Think about what you've been saying to your potential perfect customers and your community via social media, in your newsletters, in one-to-one interactions, and in passing conversations. Where can you start to sprinkle your core message?

Suggested actions:

- Write an article about something related to your core message.
- Share your core message with your nurture huddle (a.k.a. your collaborative gathering of peers) or trusted group of friends.
- Craft a few tweets inspired by your core message. Ask questions that invite others to join the conversation to help you learn more about what others think of the idea.
- Share photos of your Fantastical Freeway Billboard or your temporary tattoo.
- At the next social gathering or networking event you go to, introduce yourself using your core message.
- Start explicitly talking to your customers about the core message. Ask them how it's showing up in the work you do together or in the products you're making.
- Step into what you want to become known for by creating a manifesto that expresses your core message more fully. See the Right-Brain Entrepreneur Badge of Honor as an example of a manifesto.

As you continue to refine your message, notice how it feels to share it, and pay attention to how your people respond. The more you can confidently and authentically express what you stand for, the more you'll attract your right peeps.

# RIGHT ⭐ BRAIN entrepreneur BADGE of HONOR!

As a right-brain entrepreneur, I

⭐ Celebrate the courage it takes to follow my heart 💗 and pursue my passions;

⭐ define my own success;

⭐ embrace my intuition to help me innovate, create, and problem-solve;

⭐ inspire and empower others through my creative freedom of expression;

⭐ Live and work in alignment with **my values**;

⭐ make a positive, meaningful impact with my business;

⭐ play an important role in pioneering a new way of working that values creativity and **Right brain** genius.

RIGHT ⭐ BRAIN entrepreneur BADGE of HONOR!

CELEBRATE! courage values MEANINGFUL creativity

pioneering SUCCESS new way INSPIRE

YES! 💗💗

## MY CREATIVE WORK MATTERS

- Review your Entrepreneurial Ecosystem (particularly the center of the Business Flower).
- Design your Fantastical Freeway Billboard.
- Create a temporary tattoo to express your core message.
- Write secret love notes to your peeps.
- Start sharing your core message publicly to help you further refine it.

## LEFT-BRAIN CHECKLIST

Your left brain appreciates keeping track of the steps you've taken toward your sustained success.

- ❏ I can articulate what I'm taking a stand for in my business.
- ❏ I'm sharing my core message out in the real world.
- ❏ I'm paying attention to what resonates with my right peeps.

# Attracting, Engaging, and Learning from Your Right Peeps

## Cultivate Connection, Community, and Customers

Just as nectar attracts honeybees, your clear and compelling message developed in the previous chapter will draw your kindred spirits to you. The more often you share your message, the clearer you'll articulate what you're taking a stand for in your business overall and in relation to each product or service you launch.

And the more people you share your message with, the more widely you'll cast your net. Sure, not everyone you reach will buy from you. And that's okay. The things you offer aren't for everyone. Even if people don't buy right away, speaking their language about something relevant and helpful will at least make them curious to find out more. Through ongoing communication, interaction, and sharing, you can foster lasting relationships.

This chapter is about cultivating your community of creative cohorts, raving fans, and devoted long-term customers who continue to grow with you and refer others to you, in this way contributing to your sustainable success.

We'll talk about the different types of relationships that can lead to paying customers. We'll explore some ways to connect with and engage with your right peeps by getting out there, building your list, and targeting your communication to specific groups. And we'll touch on creating opportunities to test and explore new ideas within your community to help evolve your initial creative concepts into outstanding products or services that you can launch more broadly.

## It All Starts with Connection

*Connections* are the individual relationships you build over time. The connection can start with just one simple exchange on Twitter or with a casual conversation at an event or in line at the grocery store.

Vivienne McMaster embodies her core message, "Be Your Own Beloved," by following the same daily self-portraiture prompts that she teaches in her classes. Her growing tribe connects with her more deeply because she's sharing and learning right alongside them.

Not every connection will lead somewhere, and that's okay. Eventually some connections become fans, influential supporters, paying customers, strategic partners, or creative cohorts.

*Community* is about bringing your right peeps together. They'll tell their friends about you. They'll sing your praises. The buzz, enthusiasm, results, and stories from fans and customers often do the selling for you, which can be a nice perk. As your community develops, you may also find people who can test out your new ideas to help you refine your product.

*Customers* are the fabulous folks who buy from you. They trust that you have something beneficial to offer, and they are willing to invest. Some people may become customers right away, but most likely that conversion from connection to customer will happen over time, especially for your big-ticket offerings. In the case of a program that I offered in 2012, for example, some of the people who became paying customers for the first time had met me at networking events anywhere from five to nine years earlier.

Gaining new customers takes more time and resources than selling to existing customers. So, once you start converting raving fans into devoted customers, find ways to continue serving them over the long-term. Your repeat customers are great for your sustained success.

## Getting Out There

Later in this chapter we'll touch on email marketing as an effective strategy for building long-term relationships with your peeps. But first, let's not overlook the power of in-person connection, especially if you're still growing your business or if you're entering a brand-new market with your existing business.

"Oh no, are you talking about networking?" you may be thinking to yourself. I get it. If you're a homebody-introvert like me, you shudder at the thought of networking. Shift your energy by reframing networking into an opportunity to find and connect with your right people. This isn't about selling yourself. This is about getting to know people and building relationships. And when you're in real-time, face-to-face conversations with others, you can more readily gauge how your core message lands. This can make you feel vulnerable, but it's also a fast track to valuable feedback.

When I first quit my corporate job, I attended as many networking meetings as I could, at least a couple times per month for the first year or two. There were groups that I didn't gel with. And then there were some groups where I felt more at home. I visited those more often and eventually became involved in one at the leadership level. But even at the events that weren't the right fit, once in a while I would still make one

## LEFT-BRAIN CHILL PILL

You're not going to attract your right peeps by tweaking your website for the hundredth time or working on your business cards. You're going to attract your right peeps by being out there in the world and interacting.

## RIGHT-BRAIN BOOSTER

Remember that your right peeps want what you have to offer. Your products or services won't be for everyone, and that's okay. It's a matter of finding the right customers who want, need, and are willing to pay for the gifts you're providing. You won't know where those people are until you put your products or services out there and test.

really awesome connection that made it all worthwhile (usually with the only other kindred spirit/fish-out-of-water in the room). Even several years later I still get referrals from some of those connections.

When you're in the early stages of your business, your in-person relationships can be your home base, moral support, and referral sources. And if you're just starting to grow an online presence, friend your face-to-face pals on social media, and this will help you find pathways into your virtual community. (It's like bringing a friend to a party where you don't know anyone. You'll feel more comfortable navigating the crowd if you have your wingman.)

You may go through phases of being more outwardly focused as you connect with groups and individuals online and in person. And you may need periods of being more inwardly focused as you ground yourself in your creative process. Strike a balance that works for you so that you're expanding your reach, nurturing authentic relationships, and getting to know what your community wants and needs, while also honoring your own need for energy and the space and time required to develop your work.

We talked about getting out there and meeting people in person. Having an ongoing, regular way to connect with and engage with your peeps will help foster relationships. Whether you sell a product or a service or both, it's important to have a way to communicate with your customers in an intimate and personal manner.

Email newsletters and campaigns are a great way to establish a more direct relationship with your customers. Your peeps have said "YES!" to having you pop up in their inbox regularly. You have permission to reach out to them rather than passively waiting for them to visit your site or blog. It's personal and proactive at the same time.

It's worth saying that building your list is a longer-term strategy for building connections and community. You might not convert subscribers into customers right away. But the sooner you can start cultivating the connection and providing value to your readers, the more time you have to develop trust and relationships that can lead to referrals or sales.

You don't necessarily need a big list, depending on what you're offering. If you have high-end offerings and need only a handful of clients each quarter to meet your moola goals, you might instead focus on creating deep one-to-one relationships through more personal outreach and referrals.

If your strategy is to reach more people and sell at lower- to midrange prices, building a list can be a great tactic for you. You can start building your list wherever you are. Even if you aren't sending out regular newsletters or announcements yet, it's better to start collecting contacts now so you have them at the ready.

Rather than sending out broadcasts from your direct email account,

Ho'omalamalama Brown, a fitness instructor and creativity teacher, uses her fun, hand-drawn "to-do-odles" to plan out how she engages with her perfect customers.

use an email marketing service such as MailChimp, Constant Contact, or AWeber. These service providers give you the tools to create subscription forms, design your email templates, and send messages out to your entire list or targeted groups. And you can run reports on your email campaigns so you can better understand how your community is engaging with your email content.

## Imagine Chatting with Your Perfect Customer over a Cuppa Tea

Now, when it comes to your emails or newsletters, you may be asking, "What do I write? Will I have anything to say?"

Write your newsletters as if you're writing to one of your favorite perfect customers. Picture her sitting in front of you. You're both engaged in a heartfelt conversation over a cup of tea. Be curious about what interests her. Share ideas and insights you think will help her or resonate with her. Let your natural voice come through.

Think of it as if you're sending a "love note" to your perfect customer. Imagine your perfect customer receiving your "love note" in her inbox. When you regard it this way, the communication can feel very personal. What a great way for building a connection.

> **TIP**
>
> If you've created a Perfect Customer Portrait from chapter 4 of the *Right-Brain Business Plan* book, tape it to your monitor or display it on your desk to help you connect with your customer. And if you haven't created a Perfect Customer Portrait yet, please just move on and don't put off sending out a newsletter because you haven't completed an exercise from another book!

Include the subscriber's first name in different places within the content where you want to draw her attention or make an important point. Just as if you were speaking to someone in real life, you might say her name before something important or to emphasize something. Your email service should have a function that lets you include the first name of the subscriber in the subject line and body of the message.

## Content Ideas for Your Newsletter

Here are some suggestions for what to write about in your newsletter. Of course this is not an exhaustive list. Just some more ideas to get your inspiration going!

- Write a short article on a topic of interest. What is your community interested in? What is top-of-mind for you that would also be relevant to your readers? Keep it to about two hundred to three hundred words, or use an excerpt and link to the longer article on your blog.

- If you create art, perhaps feature a piece and share the story or symbolism behind it.

- If you teach yoga, share a pose and include a photo, description, and benefits.
- If you teach nutrition, share a recipe or highlight a food that's in season.
- If you teach a craft, share a simple pattern or a quick instructional video.
- Give your top three to five tips for addressing problems your perfect customers face.
- Keep in mind the months, seasons, and holidays for ideas on how to make your newsletter content and your product or service timely and relevant.
- Share helpful resources that your audience will benefit from — for example, talk about a quote, song, book, or movie that inspired you in your work.
- Give special previews or discounts to your subscribers.
- Announce upcoming events, shows, or class schedules.
- Feature a client.
- Provide an peek into your latest project or tell how you create your products.
- Include photos and graphics to make your newsletter visually interesting, especially if your peeps are right-brainers like you! If you don't take photos, you can use pictures from Flickr.com that are covered by the site's creative commons license. Make sure to follow the license requirements (such as giving credit and using only works okayed for commercial use).

TIP

Smartphone cameras and photo apps make it easy to take great pictures and process them in the palm of your hand. (See the resources at the back of this book for other suggested tools.)

When you're setting up your email list, consider the following:

- Place the email sign-up form in a clearly visible spot, such as the top right-hand corner (or use a pop-up window). Also, consider having the sign-up form on a separate page so you can easily link to it in your bio or guest posts.

- Include an image or thumbnail of the freebie, which can make it more real and enticing.
- State your privacy policy (no spam, no sharing contact info, and so on).
- Set up a confirmation page (or use the default one in your email system) so that subscribers see where they are in the sign-up process.
- Create a brief welcome email that subscribers immediately receive upon signing up, so that they start hearing from you right away. Include a warm thank-you for signing up, your picture so they recognize who the message is from, a link to your free gift if you promised one, assurance that they can unsubscribe whenever they want, the name of the person to contact if they have questions, how often to expect to hear from you, and any other information that may be helpful.

## A Note about Spam (Not the Kind in a Can!)

Don't add people to your list without their permission. That's considered spam. Even if you have their email addresses because they're in the email address book of your regular email account, that doesn't mean you have permission to send these people your newsletter. You can send them a message with a link, saying you're starting a list and telling them that, if they want to subscribe, they can click on the link and fill out the form.

Also, if you meet someone at a networking event and she hands you her business card, that doesn't mean you can automatically add her to your newsletter list. If it feels natural in the conversation, you can mention that you have a list and ask if you can add her. If she says yes, make a note of it on the back of her card. But if it doesn't feel natural (most of the time it probably won't — how would you like it if you shook someone's hand and she immediately said, "Hey, can I send you my newsletter?"), start building a relationship with her first.

It's really okay if people unsubscribe from your list. Really! I know you're probably fretting about people unsubscribing. Heck, you may even obsess about it after you send your newsletters out. (I did for a while!) But ultimately you're going to want people who *want* to get messages from you. The ones who are excited to hear from you every time you make contact, and who can't wait to learn about what you have in store for them next. Besides, if you're paying a per subscriber fee for those newsletters, you want people on the list who are truly interested in your work.

## Some Ways to Build Your List

Okay, so now that you have your opt-in page set up, how do you get people to it and get them to sign up? Offer them a free goodie when they sign up. You don't have to give it all away — just offer a taste! Some examples:

- A free report (in the form of a PDF)
- A short e-course delivered in, let's say, five emails
- A free MP3 of a meditation
- An audio recording of a class you gave
- A link to a video of you teaching something or being interviewed
- A short series of videos
- A free pattern, recipe, or instructions
- Free work sheets
- A fun exercise or template for making something
- The first module of a course
- A sample chapter of your book

Here are some additional creative ways to build your list:

- Offer a free live class either via teleconference or via video broadcast. People get the recording if they sign up.
- Develop a free e-book in collaboration with five to ten other people so that you get cross-promotion. Administer the sign-up/download on your site so that you capture the names. That's your perk for spearheading the collaboration, and in return you give exposure to your fellow collaborators.
- If you sell a product, offer a special one-time-only discount coupon as a thank-you for signing up.
- Run a contest or giveaway. For example, have people sign up to enter a drawing to win one of your favorite books, an item from you, or a free session with you. You could cross-promote someone else's book or prize, but be the one who administers the raffle so that you capture the names.
- Be a guest speaker on someone's podcast, radio show, tele-summit or video summit (a virtual conference held over the phone or by streaming video), or other venue and offer your free gift at the end (check with the host first to make sure promotions are allowed).
- Do a guest blog-post on a site that your perfect customers read, and provide a link to your free gift (here, too, check with the host first to make sure promotions are allowed).
- Create multiple free gifts that you develop over time and use for different purposes.
- Let people know about your free gift on social media.

When you create your free gift, make sure you include a call to action such as "Schedule a complimentary thirty-minute consultation" or "Use this coupon to get 20 percent off your next order." I don't know how many free gifts I've seen that offer so much valuable information but then leave the reader hanging, unsure of what the next step is. So make it easy for your readers by being clear about how they can get in touch with you and how they can work with you. A specific invitation is like an on-ramp that they can easily follow. You're doing them a favor

The whimsical artwork of Nicole Piar, an illustrator and surface designer who goes by the name Ghostkitten, has graced everything from greeting cards to clothes to books. Nicole created these printable list pads featuring her cute characters Sadie and Zee as a free, downloadable thank-you gift for signing up to receive her newsletter.

by being direct and specific. For more guidance in creating a free gift, see the exercises for packaging your gifts and crafting your offer, found in the next chapter.

## A Note on Schedules and Frequency

People often ask how frequently they should send out their newsletters. It's really up to you. At minimum of once a month is a good rule of thumb. Any less and your peeps will probably forget that they subscribed and may be surprised when you send out a message.

In terms of *when* to send your newsletter, again it's up to you. Some people like to send out their newsletters weekly on the same day of the week, or on a certain date, such as the first of the month or the first and fifteen, or generally twice a month but not on a fixed schedule. Having a sense of your frequency and schedule will also help you plan out your launches and promotions (which we will cover in chapter 6).

What would feel like a comfortable frequency for you? What can you commit to doing?

## Things to Track

Here are some left-brain details to consider tracking in order to better understand your list and how people are engaging with your communications. I suggest looking for overall trends. So look at the results over time, perhaps a period of three to six months, before making any major adjustments.

- Are there certain days when your subscribers are consistently more likely to open your messages? For example, are your open rates higher on Saturdays than on Mondays?
- Do certain subscriber lists have a higher open rate? If so, you may be able to convert these subscribers to paying customers more easily than those on the main list, because they are more interested in or committed to a particular topic.
- What links do people click on in the content of your message? Are there certain offers or messages, more than others, that entice people to click through to your site? Were the links formatted in a way that made them stand out more (if so, perhaps that's something you'll want to do again)?
- Notice when more people ask to be added to your list. (Is it when you offer a certain promotion? Or when you are featured on someone else's site?) This can help you identify which promotions or guest posts are more effective. You may want to repeat that action.
- A less scientific metric to track is which newsletters prompt the most direct replies to you. Did you ask readers a specific question or for feedback? If so, what kind of responses did you get, and what can you learn from that? Did you share something powerful or something that showed a particularly vulnerable side of you that really resonated with folks?
- Did you ask a question in the subject line or body of the message and include the subscriber's first name (for example, "Jane, what's your body telling you right now?")? I often get more replies back when I have subject lines like that, and people will say they really needed to hear that message just then. They felt as if it were targeted to them at just the right time.

## RIGHT-BRAIN ENTREPRENEUR SPOTLIGHT

Ho'omalamalama (Ho'o) Brown is a fitness instructor, creativity teacher, and licensed Right-Brain Business Plan facilitator. Ho'o shows us that sometimes your right peeps may be groups rather than simply individual consumers. Get creative with who you reach out to and how, since eàch audience is different.

In addition to working with clients one-on-one, Ho'o also works with local corporations and with organizations such as day care centers, independent studios, and federally funded programs. Since these existing groups often need folks to come in and run programs, she makes sure to get to know key people in these organizations so she can understand what their needs are and submit proposals. She makes herself visible within those circles by volunteering, attending their events, and supporting their community outreach.

Depending on your business, you too may want to connect with organizations or local groups or even retail stores or wholesalers. Like Ho'o, you may have a more high-touch, hands-on relationship with your business contacts than you would with a mass audience of direct consumers.

## Making It Real. Start Now!

Okay, we've just gone through a whole lot of ideas and suggestions. And even so, this list is not exhaustive — there is no one right way to go about attracting your right peeps. But by no means do you need to incorporate all these things. Especially if doing so means you'll delay sending out your first (or next) message!

## ACTION ACCELERATOR

Don't wait to reach out. Start now! Then tweak as you go. Send a newsletter out. See what readers seem to respond to, and let that help you make decisions.

## Learn from Your Right Peeps

Another way to really engage your right peeps and learn from your perfect customers is to invite a small group to test out your new idea before you launch it to a broader audience. It's a powerful way to foster fans who feel invested in you because they've gotten in on the ground floor and have contributed to your work. Moreover, you get the value of learning how you can improve your offerings.

The clearer and more direct you can be about what you want feedback on, the easier you make it for your testers to provide insight and suggestions. Simply stating, "I'd love your feedback" or "What do you think?" may feel too overwhelming for the person to answer. Of course, there may be times when keeping it open-ended is good, because you don't want to lead testers with your questions or narrow the feedback. But most times you'll probably want to know specific things.

Here are examples of questions you can ask:

- Does this make sense to you?
- What's missing?
- Is there something you could use more of?
- Are the instructions easy to follow?
- What is most valuable to you?
- What is least valuable and why?
- What results did you experience from this product or service?
- How did you feel after using the product or service?

Sure, the left-brained folks, who are less apt to take things personally, and folks who have built up a tough skin, may be able to ask for feedback and take it all with a grain of salt. Yay for them! From what I know about myself and from working with other sensitive souls, though, sharing our creative work, especially new work, can be a most disquieting experience. While it can be incredibly scary for you to share your budding idea, it's important to get outside yourself and see what others respond to.

Jen Young, owner of Spitfire Fitness Arts, created these collages to represent the types of perfect customers she likes to work with. Jen has conducted surveys of her clients to gain a deeper understanding of her perfect customers' needs.

## Create a Protective Bubble

Carve out time to look at all the feedback at one time. If you look at it as the replies come in, you can easily distract yourself and let one slightly negative comment color your whole day. Pick a time when you can center yourself and be open to receiving all the feedback. There's nothing worse than obsessing about a less-than-favorable remark and having that be counterproductive. When you are grounded and feel emotionally fortified, you are better able to look at the critiques impartially and to think about what's best for the business and the customer, rather than how your ego is reacting.

Sort through the feedback and decide what suggestions you'll act on. Remember that you don't have to use it all. Color-code the responses to help you organize your thoughts. Employ green for feedback you'll definitely use, yellow for something you'll strongly consider, and red for things you disagree with or choose to ignore.

If you start to see common themes, that's worth paying attention to. Of course, you also need to weigh what's showing up against what is right for your business. Sometimes people will have very specific feedback that really only pertains to them; and while you'll appreciate it, you won't necessarily need to act on it because it won't help the overall product or experience for other people. You can listen to what the testers say, but you can also learn from what they actually do or don't do — that is, they may say one thing but do another. So any opportunity to observe them is valuable, too. Also, you may not be able to address certain pieces of feedback with this particular offering, but you can make note of the suggestions that give you clues to a potential future version or a new product or service.

Are you procrastinating about asking for feedback or looking at feedback results? Then get an accountability buddy to report back to. Tell your buddy that you will send your feedback questions to a specific number of people by a certain date. Then, when you get results back, set a date and time to look over the responses, and let your buddy know. Make sure to report to your buddy when you've done what you promised.

## RIGHT-BRAIN BOOSTER

Before you dive into reviewing feedback, pour yourself a nice cuppa tea and have your folder with kudos and other feel-good stuff nearby. This folder is a special place where you can keep positive notes to refer to if you start to feel your confidence wavering.

Beware of getting too caught up in feedback-collection mode, because that's really just another way to hide out or stall. You're never going to satisfy everyone, and you'll never be able to perfect your product or service 100 percent. That's why you need to be clear about your own criteria while remaining open to suggestions. Go back to what's important to you and what you're trying to accomplish, and make sure your end result still meets the needs of the audience and is providing value.

The feedback you receive about how the product or service helped your early testers can turn into a case study about how your product or service helped someone. You can leverage the feedback as testimonials for your "love letter," which we'll cover in the next chapter.

## Stay Connected and Keep Providing Value

The more you can attract, engage, and learn from your right people, the easier it will be to turn your raving fans into devoted customers. So keep on finding ways to connect and provide value. Now that you've set the stage for yourself and your right peeps, you're ready to really get down to business in part III, as you learn ways to share your gifts and make more moola.

## Recap of Activities

- Get out there and connect with your right peeps.
- Start building your list.
- Send out your newsletter regularly.
- Learn from your right people by conducting tests and asking for feedback.

 **LEFT-BRAIN CHECKLIST**

Your left brain appreciates keeping track of the steps you've taken toward your sustained success.

- ❏ I am developing connections with my right peeps.
- ❏ I am finding ways to bring my right peeps together as a community.
- ❏ I am turning raving fans into devoted customers.
- ❏ I have my email-newsletter list set up, and I'm regularly sending newsletters to stay in touch with my right peeps.
- ❏ I am constantly learning from my right peeps by listening intently and testing ideas with them early on.

# PART III

# GETTING DOWN TO BUSINESS

# Packaging Your Gifts and Crafting Your Offer

## Switch from Selling to Serving

Now that you're clear on your core message and are attracting and engaging with your right people, let's look at how you'll package and sell your products and services to your perfect customers. Your business growth relies on providing something of value that people will buy and, hopefully, buy again and again.

This chapter covers how to package and share your gifts. Whether those gifts are the beautiful jewelry pieces you design, the gluten-free brownies you bake, the massage sessions you've bundled together, or sessions of the six-month boot camp you're running, you want to present your product or service in the form of an offer. An offer makes clear to prospective customers what they're getting, why they need it, and what it costs. It's like taking your product or service, wrapping it up in attractive paper, and tying it with a pretty bow to make it enticing for people to buy *now*. We'll use the metaphor of a gift to help you define all the key elements that go into your offer. And then we'll discuss how to write a sales page (a.k.a. a love letter) to communicate your offer to your perfect customers and make it easy for them to purchase. Without the offer, love letter, or launch (the latter is covered in the next chapter), your perfect customers won't know about your product or service.

The last part of this chapter takes it a step further as we explore information products (a.k.a. your bundled know-how). If you're an experienced entrepreneur who wants to package your gifts, content, and teachings to maximize your moola-making, you can jump to that section. We'll briefly touch on idea generation, content creation, and prototyping, along with my favorite right-brain tools and tips for product development.

## Revisit Your Entrepreneurial Ecosystem

This is a good time to bring out your Business Flower drawing. When you did your Entrepreneurial Ecosystem assessment, did you have enough leaves valued at the right amount to reach the moola goal on your flower stem? If not, pay special attention to this chapter. The exercises on crafting your offer will help you grow more moola-making leaves on your stem.

## Authentic Selling = Sharing Your Gifts

For as long as I've known my dear friend Julie from college, we've had a knack for getting each other just the right gift. Like when she got me that giant box of crayons for Christmas because we enjoyed scribbling in coloring books instead of studying for exams. And she knows I'm a sucker for green shirts. Sometimes I may see the perfect goodie for her, and even though her birthday may not be for months, I grab it anyway because I'm pretty sure she'll adore a cute handmade necklace.

I have a hunch there's at least one person in your life you love finding the perfect present for. Maybe you overheard her expressing to her husband how stressful work is, so you surprise her with a massage gift certificate. Or you know her favorite color is red, so you crochet her some crimson fingerless gloves.

Now, what's with all this talk about personal gift giving? Well, in order to grow your business and make more moola, you'll need to sell your products and services. But does the idea of selling your work make you cringe? If so, that's why I'd like you to remember how much you enjoy giving the perfect present to your loved one. It's way more fun and gratifying than "selling," right? Imagine if you were able to package your work into the perfect gifts for your perfect customers. And imagine offering these packages with ease.

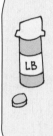

## LEFT-BRAIN CHILL PILL

Instead of fixating inward on how awkward you feel "selling" yourself, turn your focus outward to your perfect customers' wants and needs. This is about your sharing your special gifts and helping your perfect customers.

A shift in perception like that got Kerri Richardson, an intuitive life strategist and business strategist, excited about selling. She says, "Instead of seeing my offerings as 'begging for money,' I saw them for what they are — opportunities for people to have powerful experiences together, get the support they deserve, and make the changes they've longed to make. This new perspective allowed me to present my offers in a clearer, more authentic way, to focus on their benefits to my clients."

You're able to get the perfect gift for your friend because you know her really well. You know what she likes and dislikes, what she wants and needs. You're aware of the significant life events and transitions she's experiencing, the struggles she's overcoming, and the accomplishments she wants to celebrate. When you're tuned into your customers in that same attentive way, as we talked about in chapter 4, you'll have a much better sense of the perfect gift that would help them, as well as how to communicate to them in a love letter the benefits of your offer.

## What Goes Into Your Offer

The following are the main elements that go into crafting your offer. (I've added references to other chapters in this book to help you, along with a few exercises from *The Right-Brain Business Plan* that may provide supplemental insight.)

- Your passions and gifts. What are you super excited about sharing with your peeps? What are you taking a stand for? (See chapter 3 of this book and your Business Self-Portrait from *The Right-Brain Business Plan*.)
- The "to" card. Who will buy your offer? Who is your perfect customer? (See chapter 4 of this book and your Perfect Customer Portraits from *The Right-Brain Business Plan*.)
- The benefits. How does this offer help your customers?
- The features. Describe what they'll be getting.
- Customer concerns or objections. Anticipate customers' concerns, and address them up front. (See chapter 4 of this book and the "barriers" sections from the Business Landscape play sheet found in *The Right-Brain Business Plan*.)
- The price. How much will the offer cost? (See chapter 7.)
- The left-brain details. Explain any fine print, including policies and procedures. (See chapter 9.)

You can use the Packaging Your Gifts play sheet to write down your ideas for each element.

NOTE: At the end of this chapter, you'll reference these elements again when you write your love letter to communicate your offer to your perfect customers, so keep them handy.

As you go through the rest of this chapter, choose one product or service for your offer, even if you have lots of ideas for various products and services. That will keep things simple and easy. Once you get the hang of what goes into an offer and writing a love letter, you can cycle through the exercises again to write your other offers. Remember, you don't necessarily need to make a lot of different offers to hit your moola goal if you sell enough of the ones you have at the right price. Also, keep in mind that the next chapter will guide you through launching your offer, and through mapping out your launches for the year if you have multiple offers.

## Your Passions and Gifts

Your products and services embody your passions and unique gifts. For the particular offer you're defining in this exercise, identify the specific product or service you're choosing to package.

Write a brief description or the title of this product or service somewhere on the gift box.

## Who Will Buy Your Offer: Target Your Perfect Customers

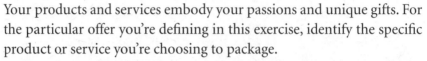

If you're trying to be too many things to too many people, your perfect customers won't recognize that the offer is meant for them. Who are you helping with this particular offer?

In the "to" tag, identify the perfect customer you're targeting with this offer.

## The Benefits: How Your Offer Will Help Your Perfect Customer

Your potential customers want to hear how your product or service is going to help them. You know — the "What's in it for me?" question. So make sure you're clearly communicating how your offer makes their situation better. Include specific results. Here are some questions to consider:

- What problem are you solving for them?
- What need are you fulfilling?
- What are you helping to make better for them? For example, are you helping them improve any of the following?
  - Personal life
  - Professional life
  - Relationships
  - Business
  - Health and fitness

- Finances
- Physical environment
- Personal style or appearance
- Creative flow
- Mental and emotional health

Decribe your customers' current situation in detail. What are they thinking and feeling right now about the challenges they're facing? Where do they want to be instead, and how will it feel to get there? How specifically will your offer get them there?

Write your responses to these questions on the benefits card.

## The Features: Describe What They'll Get

Your customers need a good understanding of what they will receive. Otherwise, they'll be confused, which will most likely keep them from buying. So what exactly will you offer them? Is it a physical product, a digital product, a service, or a program? Is it a combination of product and service?

### Is Your Offer a Physical Product? Is It a Handmade Good?

If so, what are the features of the item? What things might be included? How many do they get? Are there different sizes, colors, or other choices? What is it made out of, and how is that, too, a benefit? How big is it — what are the dimensions? How much does it weigh?

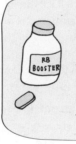

**RIGHT-BRAIN BOOSTER**
Emphasize emotion. When it comes to compelling benefits, painting a visceral picture helps your potential customer say, "Yes! That's me! I need that!"

### Is Your Offer a Program, Service, or Information Product?

What's included? How long is it? How many sessions? How will the content or service be delivered to the customer? For example, is it a class, a digital information product, a workshop, in-person sessions over the phone, or a video chat? Are there different modules or supplemental materials?

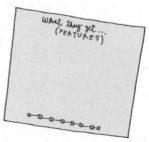

# RIGHT BRAIN, THEN LEFT BRAIN:
## BENEFITS FIRST, FOLLOWED BY FEATURES

A description of benefits helps customers feel and experience how the offer will improve their situation. The features should be itemized so that customers understand exactly what they're getting. But start with compelling, emotional benefits first to draw them in.

### Handmade-Good Example

If you were selling a handmade bag, you might point out these *benefits*:

- The bag will help your customer express her individuality, since no two bags are alike.
- It's both stylish and good to the environment.
- It's a fashionable way to carry her laptop or to pack for a weekend getaway.
- Sturdy design makes this bag durable for everyday use.
- Purchasing this bag supports local artisans.

And *features* might include these points:

- Handmade out of recycled wool sweaters
- Measures 18" wide x 13.5" tall x 5" deep
- Comes in a choice of blues and greens or oranges and yellows
- Features recycled-wood buttons as embellishments

### Program, Service, or Information Product Example

If you were selling an "Intro to Yoga" workshop, *benefits* might include these:

- If you've felt embarrassed attending yoga classes because you didn't know what you were doing, you'll feel safe and comfortable in our caring, nonjudgmental environment.
- You'll receive personal attention from a seasoned yoga instructor to ensure correct alignment and avoid injury.
- Learn the foundation for a beginning yoga practice in one day — perfect for those with a busy weekday schedule.

And *features* might be:

- A one-day workshop from 10 AM to 5 PM on the first Saturday of the month
- An overview of and instruction in sun salutations and basic standing poses in the morning and seated poses in the afternoon
- A handout with photos and descriptions of basic poses
- A free pass to a one-hour yoga class to be used within thirty days

## Anticipate Customer Concerns or Objections
## and Nip Them in the Bud

When you're engaged with your community, as we talked about in chapter 4, you have a sense of what their questions may be and where there may be resistance to making an investment or commitment. What reasons might your perfect customers have to say "No, thanks" or "Not right now," and how can you address them ahead of time?

For example, if you foresee that your customers may say, "I don't have enough money right now to pay for this," one way to address that in advance is to offer payment plans so that each installment is within a customer's monthly budget.

Turn a potential concern into an unexpected benefit. For example, if you're offering a virtual event, some people may think it will be too impersonal. But you can emphasize that deeper connections can happen in the chat room because individuals can have instantaneous interactions with fellow participants, unlike at an in-person gathering, where they must wait for a scheduled break.

Anything that raises questions or doubts can get in the way of a purchase. By anticipating and addressing possible objections ahead of time, you show your right peeps that you understand what's in their hearts and minds, you help alleviate their apprehension, and you make it that much easier for them to say yes. Write your responses to these questions on the concerns card you've created.

## Set Your Price

Setting your price can be one of the more challenging aspects of the offer. However, it's important for you to be clear about the number so that you can communicate it with ease and certainty to your perfect customers. If you hesitate or muddle your way through stating the cost, they may lose confidence in you.

Ultimately, you need to come to a number that

- feels good to you;
- covers your costs and then some, so you can make a healthy profit;

- enables you to feel you're providing the appropriate value (you're not overselling yourself); and
- is acceptable to your customers.

Finding that sweet spot can take some exploration and experimentation. See chapter 7, pages 129–31, for more discussion on pricing.

Do you offer special rates? Do prices go up after a certain date? Is there a payment plan? Does it make sense to have one simple price, or would you reach more of your perfect customers if you had tiered pricing? For example, could you offer a low-cost entry-level option, a midlevel option, and a high-level, VIP option?

Write your responses to these questions in the price tag and fill in the price(s) you will charge.

## Define the Left-Brain Details

Don't forget to be clear about the details of your offer. We'll cover these types of policies and procedures in chapter 9, so you can jump there for more specific considerations. But for now, here are a few examples of particulars you should clearly explain to your customers.

How will your customers pay you? Online via credit card or PayPal? Will you accept only checks? If so, who should the checks be made out to, and where do they send them? Are there certain deadlines or restrictions? Will you accept returns and give refunds? Will you offer a money-back guarantee? How will they receive your product or service? What's the shipping cost? Who can they contact with further questions?

Not having these details spelled out can raise customer concerns, so communicate them up front.

Write your responses to these questions on the left-brain details card.

## Tie It All Up with a Pretty Bow

What will make your offer absolutely irresistible to your perfect customers and make your heart sing? What bells and whistles will make your offer a must-have, a no-brainer for them to purchase? Think of a good complement to your offer — what will add to the experience without overwhelming the customer?

Here are some ideas for bonuses, pretty bows, and bells and whistles:

- A book, CD, or movie related to the theme of the product or service
- An accessory to go with the purchase, such as a key chain for a purse or a journal to go with a course
- A VIP ticket to an event
- A bring-a-friend discount
- A promise that a portion of the proceeds will go to a cause that resonates with you and your perfect customers
- A one-month free subscription to, or a supply of, something
- A gift certificate or freebie from a complementary vendor
- A one-hour session with you
- A report or article related to the product or service
- A discount on future offers

Sometimes bells and whistles can be too much, and adding them diminishes the value of the offer by detracting from what the customer ultimately will get out of it. And if you add too many bonuses, your offer will look confusing and disjointed. Going back to the gift metaphor, it would be like wrapping up a birthday gift in garish Christmas paper, adorning it with a Halloween-style black-and-orange bow, and topping it off with a Valentine's Day heart. Those bells and whistles are meant for different occasions and clearly don't go together. My mentorship cohorts jokingly refer to this monstrosity as the "omni gift." Don't offer the omni gift!

Remember to keep things simple and focused. That will make things easier not only for you the creator but also for your customers. You don't have to do it all, include it all, or otherwise overextend yourself. A small and simple brown paper package tied up with string may be the perfect gift.

Write your ideas for bonuses on the top of the box with the bow. These are things that will make your offer simply irresistible to your perfect customers.

Keep in mind that sometimes it's worth putting in the extra time and effort to customize a unique program, product, or experience for your elite customers, rather than just offering them your standard "off-the-shelf" products or services. Perhaps it's a high-end commissioned art piece or a special six-month, individualized nutrition program that includes weekly home-cooked meals, a package that will go for thousands of dollars.

Also, be listening for opportunities to offer something on the spot. Once in a while you may find yourself in a conversation with someone who learns about what you do and says, "I need that!" Even if you don't have something in your ready-to-go gift collection, find a way to understand what this person's needs are and craft something for him then or make sure to follow up with him right away. Of course, do this only if you do indeed want to work with him. But I bet there have been times when you missed out on offering a sale to someone who was totally ready to work with you or buy something from you. That's why it can be helpful to have some offers ready to go and to be comfortable with making different ones to meet your customers' needs.

## Communicate the Offer:
## Love Letters to Your Perfect Customers

This chapter on packaging your gifts helps you determine the elements that go into your offer. The notes you've written so far will help you write your sales page (a.k.a. a love letter) to communicate your offer to your perfect customers. Your love letter gives them a place to say YES to your gifts and to easily make a purchase.

The love letter I refer to pertains to more than a typical sales page. It could also be a product listing on a website or Etsy, a brochure or pamphlet, a physical letter or flyer you send in the mail, a personal and direct email to someone

## RIGHT-BRAIN BOOSTER
To get your creativity flowing and to make a personal connection, handwrite a note to your perfect customer as a first draft. That'll be sure to get you in the love letter mode.

who has already expressed interest in working with you, a broadcasted email message to your list, an ad in a local publication, or even a sign-up sheet or order form that you place on a table at your event (if it's an order form, make sure it includes a section to collect their contact and payment info). Various sections of the love letter's content may also live in parts of your main website (for example, in an "Is This You?" page that helps readers know if they are your type of customer).

There will be times when your perfect customer won't see the love letter and instead will speak with you directly. Even so, the exercise of writing the love letter will help you practice articulating the offer so that you can make the sale easily and effortlessly.

## RIGHT-BRAIN ENTREPRENEUR SPOTLIGHT

Kerri Richardson, the intuitive life strategist and business strategist I mentioned earlier, was expanding her successful individual coaching practice by adding group coaching. She needed to fill her programs, and she wanted to speak authentically while making her pitch.

Kerri said, "I never liked the idea of a sales page, but a love letter? Oh, I can write that. This shift literally took me from struggling to get a page done to banging one out in half a day. Being a naturally compassionate person, I loved the idea of sharing tools to help people through their challenges. Writing it from that place felt awesome!"

With that initial love letter, Kerri sold out her first group coaching program! So — you guessed it — she continues to repeat what works, and each new love letter gets easier to write.

### Anatomy of a Love Letter

I've included a diagram of a love letter to help you see how all the pieces fit together. You don't need to include all these points, however, or follow this particular order. Add as much detail as needed. If you're offering something free to gain exposure and build your list, or a low-priced item, you probably don't need as much information as you would for a higher-ticket offer.

# Anatomy of a Sales Page

**A.K.A.** Love Letter

## DEAR "PERFECT CUSTOMER",

A greeting that your peeps will identify with.
For example: "Dear Hardworking parent"
(or Creative Soul or overwhelmed business owner.)

Help your peeps say, "Hey! That's me!!!"

### WELCOME message

Some examples include:

- tell your personal story
  - why this matters to you

- An "Is this You?" header followed by Descriptions they can easily relate to.

- Why they need to read on...

Your beautiful headshot

put your pic on the page so people can immediately connect with you.

Name + title
Connection and credibility

Use powerful, vivid images that paint a compelling picture of your offer.

**★ INCLUDE CATCHY CAPTION**

## ☆ BENEFITS ☆

☆ How are you making their lives better?
☆ How are you addressing their needs/challenges?
☆ How will this rock their world?

**" SUMMARIZE TESTIMONIAL WITH A SHORT HEADLINE "**

Include terrific testimonials!
Have them focus on the left-brain **RESULTS**
(#s, %, outcomes) & the right-brain BENEFITS
(softer outcomes, emotion, story)
MIX of BOTH. BOLD key phrases.

Social proof adds to your credibility.

NAME. TITLE.
LOCATION AND/OR BIZ

→ Sprinkle throughout

# CALL TO ACTION

What Do you want them to Do? Sign up? Buy now? And by when?

## PRICE:
include How much it costs and any special rates or early-bird Discounts.

**BUY NOW** — make it easy to purchase

## WHAT THEY GET : FEATURES

| | OPTION 1 | OPTION 2 |
|---|---|---|
| FEATURE 1 | ✓ | ✓ |
| FEATURE 2 | ✓ | ✓ |
| FEATURE 3 | | ✓ |
| FEATURE 4 | | ✓ |
| PRICE | $ | $$ |

A left-brain table clearly communicates options

What's included?
- ⭐ product — materials, Dimensions, weight, how many pieces, color choices, etc.
- ⭐ service/program — topics, how many sessions, types of sessions, how long? etc.
- ⭐ any special bonuses

## FAQs
- Help answer or address any of the potential objections ahead of time.
- Cover some of the left-brain logistics

## CLOSING / parting words
- include some final thoughts & a personal note
- what you're taking a stand for
- what you really, really want for them.

happiness, Success, Freedom...

### FINAL CALL TO ACTION:
Don't forget: " purchase by xx Date to get the special Bonus!!"

♥, your name

NOW GO FORTH. SEND YOUR LOVE LETTER INTO THE WORLD. ♥

## Dear Hardworking Parent,

Parenting is hard, hard, HARD work.

When you try to parent fully awake, eyes wide open, mindful of your choices, life gets intense.

Your child — 6 months old, toddler, 4 years old, teenager, off to college, gone and married — is pushing you to expand in uncomfortable ways into unknown territory. **Some days you make mistake after mistake.** You work hard, and still you feel like a failure as a parent. Maybe you go to bed thinking, "Geez, I gotta do better tomorrow."

Feeling alone, overwhelmed, or confused on your parenting journey?

### The reality: We are becoming just like our parents.

We work hard to find our way, a new way. Yet we are wired to do the very thing we do not wish to do. Research shows that despite our best efforts, we still parrot old ways, the ways we learned from our own experience.

There's good news: Research also shows we can **transform old ways** through the hard, yet simple, work of **awareness, presence, and vulnerability**.

*You can rewire yourself for connection to what really matters to you.*

## Ready to rewire? Click here to sign up now.

### Is this for you?

Coaching Circles are for you IF you want to:

- Stop thinking and start feeling more **gentle, patient, and positive**
- Have **practical tools** for more ease, peace, rhythm, and cooperation
- Get **community and guidance** that help you move through the hard parts of change in safety
- Come to your own conclusions and **make your own choices**

Go from exhausted to excited about parenting with coaching and community support.

### Why does it matter?

1. Our "problems" aren't going to go away.
2. Despite any mistakes you've made so far, you can start to be the parent you want to be.
3. More ease, more flow, more safety, more joy = deeper, faster, BIGGER results.

Here is a real-world example of a sales page based on Sheila Pai's love letter promoting her parenting coaching circles. This gives an idea of how you can incorporate different elements of the love letter into your offer.

How do I know it's possible to shift? Because I've come through it and now share all I learned with you....

I was yelled at as a child. I had self-hating and life-fearing beliefs planted deep within me. This affected my parenting.

As a new mom of two, I set out in earnest to fully rewire myself for peace and connection — and I believe you can, too!

I eventually *did* find a way not only to survive but to thrive, as a whole family.

Only, I had to do it alone...
...and I am committed to ensuring that you have everything you need to do it on your own AND in community.

## THE DETAILS
### 12 Weeks of Coaching Circles

What you get:

- What makes shift possible: 12 calls of live coaching, live community, and conscious listening
- How to keep things moving: 12 weeks of resources and support through email
- Access when you need it most: Ongoing community forum and downloadable handouts for easy reference

When: Live calls Sundays, 8:30 p.m. EST

Price: $329 • Early-bird price: $269

*What are people saying about time with me?*

"I am able to **connect more positively with my children**, while recognizing and accepting my own personal limits and values. Through the mothers' circles, I have an **outlet to be honest about my parenting** and personal struggles and successes. Investing in my parenting through these circles has been **one of the most important things I have done for myself**." (Nancy, PA)

"Your empathy is very helpful, very encouraging. You do a great job of finding the positive and building mamas up. You are offering mothers **a gift for generations to come**." (Jennifer, NJ)

Sheila Pai is founder of A Living Family, which provides parenting, relationship, and life coaching.

## Ready to rewire? Click here to sign up now.

P.S. If you are not yet a parent and could use this guidance, I encourage you to get support now in preconception so your efforts can go even farther, instead of having to unlearn things in the heat of the moment. Get in touch and let me know you're ready to rewire.

**Just like in Sheila's example, you don't need to include all of the love letter elements that are mentioned in this book. Simply choose the sections that are most important for your message.**

*Who Is Your Love Letter To?*

Dear "Perfect Customer" — start with a welcome or greeting using words and descriptions your people will identify with. For example, you might begin with "Dear business owner" (or *creative soul, stressed-out parent*, or *overworked employee*, whatever will help your peeps say, "Hey, that's me!").

*What Your Welcome Message Could Include*

- A short, personal story
- Questions that help illustrate the pain your customers are experiencing or the gap between where they are now and where they want to be
- A personal video intro
- An "Is this you?" header followed by some descriptions they can relate to
- Why they should read on

What challenges are they are having? What are their pain points? What are they missing in their lives or businesses? How can you paint the picture for them (and are there photos to help paint that?) so that they see themselves?

Put a professional photo of yourself at the top of the page so people can immediately connect with you. This could be a nice, friendly head-shot, or an action shot of you doing your work, or a photo of you with your product.

Use powerful, vivid images to paint a picture of what you have to offer. Top them off with catchy captions that entice the reader. Some ideas for images:

- You with a client
- You designing or making your products
- You at a show or event with your vendor table
- You teaching
- Your products
- Your happy customers with your product

- Metaphors that relate to the message of your offer
- The location where the event will be held so people can picture themselves there

Sometimes you might need to rely on stock photos, but your original high-quality images will best convey your brand and message.

## Benefits

Be specific and clear about how you're addressing your potential customers' needs or challenges. A bulleted list is easier for potential customers to read or skim. Use boldface for key words or phrases that pack a punch.

Use descriptive and emotional language — being a right-brainer gives you an advantage in writing compelling copy. Engage the senses; get into the shoes of your perfect customers and imagine what their lives are like.

## Include Terrific Testimonials

Make each customer quote easy to skim by including a short headline that summarizes the rave review. For maximum impact include both *left-brain results*, like numbers, percentages, and tangible outcomes, and *right-brain benefits*, such as the softer, more emotional outcomes and personal stories. Here, too, emphasize the most powerful points by using boldface for key words and phrases in the testimonial.

Include a photo of each customer whose testimonial you use, as well as the person's name, title, location, business, and any other information that would be relevant. This gives the testimonials more credibility and helps potential customers relate to them. They'll ask themselves, "Are these people like me?" Testimonials add to your credibility. They are social proof that what you have to offer works. The

Meditation teacher and life coach Bindi Shah created a collaged box to help design her group-coaching circle offer. The images remind her of the positive difference she wants to make in the participants' lives and the index cards organize content for the program.

**TIP**

Brainstorm some catchy captions, headlines, and compelling questions to spice up your love letter. Let your peeps know how much you care about them, understand them, and want to help them. Your pic can be another way to make the letter end on a more personal note.

implicit message in them is: "See people just like you who get results." You can place the testimonials all in one section or sprinkle them throughout.

If you have a new product or service to offer, consider doing test runs or providing samples to people beforehand to gather testimonials. As we talked about in chapter 4, it's great to get early feedback and customer insight while you're developing something, and chances are you'll have some good quotes to use from that phase of development.

You can also leverage testimonials from your other work as long as they convey the essence of what you're providing. You can top them with a header like: "What people have said about working with me" or "What people have said about my other programs" or "Hear how much people love my other products."

## Call to Action

What do you want the person reading to do? Do you want her to buy now? Sign up for a class, an individual session, a consultation? Refer a friend to you? Be clear about what you're specifically asking for.

Include images that emphasize the action you want potential customers to take. And add a call to action in various places on the page, including the top and bottom — make it easy to buy or sign up!

## Features

Describe what the customers will get.

Some product feature examples include:

- What materials is the product made out of?
- What are the dimensions and weight?
- What are the color choices?
- How many pieces do they get?

Some program or service features include:

- What are the topics?
- How many sessions?
- How long is the program or service? When does it run?
- How is the program or service delivered? An in-person class, over the phone, or online?

If you need to describe various options, a left-brain table can help to clearly communicate features, prices, and options. For example, where you discuss price, clearly state how much your offer costs. Include specials, early-bird discounts, and options and add a "buy now" button.

### FAQs

A list of frequently asked questions can answer possible objections readers may have ahead of time. Use this list to reiterate the left-brain details such as logistics, guarantees, and policies. Make sure you include the name of the person to contact with questions and how to get in touch.

## ACTION ACCELERATOR
Make your offer to two to three people right now. Pick up the phone and call some individuals who have already expressed interest in working with you, and invite them to sign up for your offer. Or send an email to your favorite clients and include a brief love letter.

### Your Bio or a Little Bit about the Company

Do they know why you're the right person to buy from? Let them know by adding your bio and your own experiences related to your product or service, whatever establishes your credibility.

Make it personable. Mention something entertaining about yourself that will help people connect to you on a personal level and show that you walk your talk. If this is a web page, people may land only on this page and won't explore the rest of your site, so make sure they know a little bit about you and your company.

Even if you already included a photo of yourself at the top of the page, add another one at the end to anchor their connection with you.

*Closing/Parting Words*

Include some final thoughts about why your product or service is so important. Reiterate what you're taking a stand for and what you want for your peeps. This is a love letter, after all, so it needs to show your heart and soul. Give it a thoughtful and powerful wrap-up.

## Productize Your Service and Bundle Your Know-How into Information Products

If you're a service provider, such as a web designer, massage therapist, hair stylist, yoga instructor, photographer, life coach, consultant, or therapist, I bet you have moments when you feel trapped in a money-for-time box. The only way to make more moola is to work with more clients. Yet there are only so many hours in a day and only so many offers you can make.

Even an artist or other maker who creates things by hand — such as a painter, crafter, potter, jewelry designer, illustrator, sewer, knitter, or pie maker — may feel the limitations of selling only as fast as her pretty pair of hands can make something.

If you're an established money-for-time service provider, or artisan who creates only handmade pieces, you may want to consider maximizing your moola-making by creating information products, which is represented in the far-right column of the Multiple Moola-Making Methods Map on page 134. It's a great way to supplement the income you earn from the direct work you do for individual customers, and it can help expand your reach. In the next section we'll explore the types and benefits of information products you can create.

If you're still relatively new to your business and don't have a fan base yet, you're probably better off focusing on your fastest path to cash first (most likely your work with individual customers) while you build products on the side. In chapter 7, we'll talk more about the things to consider when it comes to diversifying your moola-making methods.

# Information Products:
## The Next Best Thing to Cloning Yourself

Do you find yourself saying the same things over and over to your clients? Do customers constantly ask you, "How did you do that?" or "Will you show me how to make that?" or "What's the secret to your success?" If so, you can package your teachings into an information product. Know-how bundles such as e-books, e-courses, and kits let you be in more than one place at once so you can help more people, in less time, while you make more moola and get known as a thought leader to boot.

Offering information products makes it easy for curious customers to get a taste of you before investing in higher-end offerings. You become more widely accessible without having to pack your calendar with individual client meetings or coffee dates. And information products can help build your credibility because you're seen as an expert. My visibility began to increase even with my first tangible information product (my Unfolding Your Life Vision kit helped me land a spot on TV because I had a visual to show), and since then my info offerings have landed me more speaking gigs and guest interviews, which put me in front of more of my right peeps.

There are different kinds of information products, and I'll touch on some briefly to give you ideas. Know-how bundles can be digital or tangible, and there are pros and cons to each.

### Digital Products

These can include, but are not limited to,

- e-books;
- downloadable patterns, simple instructions, and tutorials for your craft;
- audio recordings such as meditations, visualizations, guest interviews, and teachings, either on their own or in addition to other multimedia pieces (great for people to listen to on the go);
- video tutorials, lessons, and demonstrations, either on their own or in addition to other multimedia pieces (great for

providing information that is best delivered with a visual component showing examples, walking through a step-by-step process, or creating an immersive, experiential session);

- recordings of live in-person or virtual workshops that can then be turned into downloadable products for people who were unable to attend the live sessions;
- e-courses — programs that you run during a scheduled time or that you package into a self-study program; and
- telesummits or video summits, where you conduct a series of interviews with guest experts and sell the recordings.

## Some Pros and Cons of Digital Products

### Pros:

- They can be faster to launch because there isn't a physical production aspect.
- They're easier to update and revise.
- The production cost is usually lower.
- Such products can be distributed faster because people download them.
- Customers experience instant gratification instead of waiting for a shipment.

### Cons:

- Because the barrier to entry is low, there are a lot of information products out there, so the marketplace is crowded.
- You must meet technology requirements for creating the product, and must have a back-end system to make the purchasing and downloading process simple. You need to have your Smooth Sailing Systems in place.
- Once customers download the product, they can't "return" it.
- Digital items can be harder to display and sell at a vendor table or in the back of the room when you do a speaking gig.

## Tangible Products Based on Your Content

Tangible information products are physical items that need to be produced, stocked, and distributed. Examples can include, but are not limited to,

- books;
- kits that include supplies and instructions;
- patterns with supplies and instructions;
- journals;
- individual cards or card decks;
- prints of artwork or photos;
- workbooks;
- binders or manuals;
- DVDs or CDs; and
- any items that have your licensed content or artwork on them (such as mugs, calendars, office supplies, shirts, bags).

## Some Pros and Cons of Tangible Information Products

*Pros:*

- They can serve as your "better" business card because they give potential customers a richer taste of your work.
- Customers can touch them, which can make it easier for them to decide to buy.
- In a world where so much is online, something you can hold in your hands can feel more special and valuable.
- They are easier to display and sell at a vendor table or at the back of the room when you speak.
- They're easier for people to purchase as gifts for others.

*Cons:*

- The cost of raw materials can be high, and you must purchase in bulk to get better rates.
- Production is usually more expensive, complex, and time-intensive.

- You must deal with physical assembly, which can be tedious and time-consuming.
- Managing inventory and handling shipping: If your volume is relatively low you may be able to assemble and ship products on your own or get a volunteer or low-cost hired hand to help you. Or you can outsource to a professional fulfillment company; but since that can be expensive, you must factor it into your price.

### EXERCISE
### Generate Ideas for Your Product

When it comes to figuring out what you want to sell or to package into a product, there are plenty of ways to generate ideas. Some key sources are: what your perfect customers have told you (circle back to chapter 4 for ideas), and what you're taking a stand for in your business (circle back to chapter 3 if needed).

Here are some questions to reflect on. Journal your responses to the prompts that spark ideas for you, and then look for themes. You can also check out the sidebar for right-brain tools for idea generation.

- What do your perfect customers need the most help with?
- What specific knowledge do you want to share with others? Or what do people ask you about all the time? What are you saying to your clients over and over again?
- What are your special gifts, your superpower or secret sauce?
- What do you wish was out there that doesn't exist right now?

Make sure that what you create will be valuable to your perfect customers. Even if you're totally enamored with your idea, ask yourself: Would someone else want this? What specifically will people get out of this? We'll cover testing those questions in the prototype section that follows and in the section on crafting your offer, later in this chapter.

# RIGHT-BRAIN TOOLS FOR IDEA GENERATION

Here are some of my favorite creative tools for getting my thoughts on paper.

*Colorful index cards.* Write an idea or word on each card, color-code them, and move the cards around until you find the right order, groupings, or themes.

*Sticky notes.* Brain-dump your thoughts onto sticky notes and attach them to a large piece of paper. Sort your ideas, using the sticky notes the same way you would index cards. Unlike cards, however, the sticky notes will stay where you put them — so you can pin them up or transport them while they're still laid out on the paper.

*Mind maps.* Draw a circle in the middle of a piece of paper. Write an idea in the circle and then draw spokes that branch off with related ideas.

*Random images.* Flip through a magazine and randomly select a page with a picture. See if that picture sparks a new idea or a new way of thinking about your current idea. Write about the new perspective.

*Free-form, stream-of-consciousness journaling.* Always keep a notebook nearby so you can capture those stray thoughts that pop into your head when you least expect it.

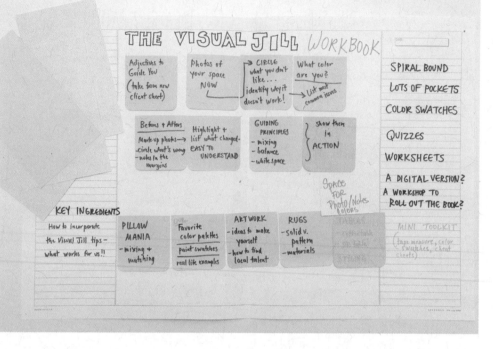

The team at Visual Jill, an interior design company, used sticky notes on a large piece of paper to sketch out an idea for a design workbook. They are testing and fine-tuning aspects of their step-by-step guide by using a prototype during initial discovery meetings with their clients.

## Create Content for Your Information Product

Now that you've landed on an idea for your information product, start making it real by creating your content. Give yourself permission to have a completely crappy, totally nonsensical first draft. Shooting for perfection right outta the gate will only keep you stuck and frustrated.

Rather than start from a blank page, repurpose and recycle. Grab existing content from your journal entries, blog posts, social media updates, newsletter articles, emails to clients, class outlines or handouts, doodles in your sketchbook, talking points from a speaking gig, or even those sticky notes on your monitor, and pull from that. Group the information, rework it, and add to it. You may find you don't even have to add much to it, other than what's needed to thread it all together.

Select a structure that supports your content. If it's a how-to guide, include your expert, step-by-step instructions. If it's an e-course, build out your teachings module by module. Use your right-brain creativity to find a format that best conveys your message. For example, when I created *Playtime with Your Inner Muse*, my e-book about intuitive painting, I knew that I wanted it to be organic and colorful, so I chose to handwrite and paint the pages.

Move back and forth from paper to pixels. The tactile, hands-on nature of paper and pen allows you to get messy and engage with your thoughts in a more tangible way. Then, when you're ready to structure, edit, or implement your ideas, transition to the computer, where it's easier to search for key words, manipulate information, and refine your content.

Kiala Givehand of Giving Hands Creative developed her first tangible product, the Mixed Media Inspiration Deck, by starting off with a simple prototype to organize her ideas. When she launched her deck, she collaborated with other mixed-media artists in a "blog hop," where she guest-posted on their blogs and hosted a fun giveaway to generate buzz.

Create content through collaboration. Inviting people to join forces with you creates built-in accountability, because others are counting on you to do your part. This approach works well when you're corralling experts to interview as part of a video summit or telesummit or partnering with a cohort to coauthor an e-book. See chapter 8 for ideas on finding the right strategic partners to collaborate with.

## Play with Prototypes

The next stage in developing your information product is to bring it to life with a prototype. When you have something tangible that you can play with, you gain new insights into what works and what doesn't. Moreover, people can test a prototype and give you valuable feedback about what needs improvement, or even ideas about a different usage. For ideas on how to gather feedback on your prototype, refer to chapter 4, pages 65–67, and to the "Launch, Then Create" section in chapter 6.

Prototypes can take many forms, such as physical mock-ups, sketches, or even storyboards. To make a storyboard, draw squares like those in a comic strip. In the first square, doodle and write what happens at the beginning of the process, and then build out the progression in the other squares.

When I knew I wanted to write a book, I took one of my handmade journals and transformed the covers into a mock-up of my future book to inspire me. I put one of my business postcards on the front cover. Then I made a back cover complete with the book's description, a fictitious quote from the *San Francisco Chronicle*, and a future bio for myself with credentials that didn't yet exist but which then came true a few years later. By letting me hold my "book" in my hands, my prototype made the idea real for me.

## LEFT-BRAIN CHILL PILL

Don't discredit all your scribbles and sticky notes. Those are pieces of the puzzle that will make up your content. Use them to spark your idea generation and content creation.

As you move from prototype to design to producing the final product, check out some of the processes mentioned in chapter 9, starting on page 184. And don't forget to take your information product through the offer and love-letter formats, too.

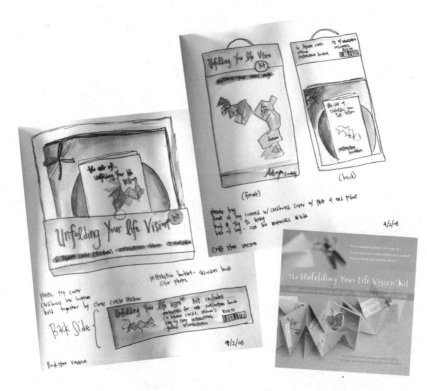

An early prototype of my Unfolding Your Life Vision kit included a sketch of packaging ideas. Ultimately the drawing helped me figure out what would go into the design of the kit booklet. I also tested the instructions in my booklet to make sure the steps were clear.

## Get Your Gifts Out There

Whether you're packaging your existing products and services into offers and love letters, or you're turning your teachings into information products to maximize your moola-making, the key is to get your gifts out there. So let's move on to the next chapter to learn how to launch your offer into the world.

- Revisit your Entrepreneurial Ecosystem (in particular, the leaves on your stem).
- Complete the Packaging Your Gifts illustrated play sheet.
- Draft your love letter.
- *More advanced:* Generate new ideas for your information product.
- *More advanced:* Create the content and prototype for your information product and test it.

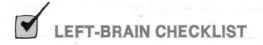

## LEFT-BRAIN CHECKLIST

Your left brain appreciates keeping track of the steps you've taken toward your sustained success.

- ❏ I have a defined product or service that I want to offer my perfect customers.
- ❏ I have articulated the benefits my perfect customers will receive from this offer.
- ❏ I have described the features included in the offer.
- ❏ I have proactively addressed potential concerns that my perfect customers may have with this offer.
- ❏ I have set the price for the offer, as well as outlined any payment plans, discounts, or specials.
- ❏ I have defined the left-brain details of the offer, such as policies, shipping, and so on.
- ❏ I have drafted my love letter to perfect customers to communicate offers and to make it easy for them to buy.
- ❏ I have shared my offer with at least two people.
- ❏ *More advanced:* I have generated ideas for an information product.
- ❏ *More advanced:* I have created some content and a prototype for my information product and am testing it.

#  6 Let's Do Launch

## Campaigns, Communications, and Calendars to Promote Your Offers

Now that you've packaged your special gifts, let's make sure your right people know about what you have to offer. It's time to get launching!

First, let's go over some ideas and approaches for using targeted launches to get the word out about your offers. Even though I'll share some left-brain tips, there isn't a step-by-step, cookie-cutter approach to launching. And besides, you're a one-of-a-kind creative entrepreneur who wants to do things in your own unique, authentic way, right? How you approach your launch really depends on what you're selling, your goals, your timing, your message, and who your audience is. You get to use your right-brain creative license to make the launch yours and to make it fun for yourself and your customers.

To give you a sense of what to consider and plan for, we'll talk about what goes into the different phases of launching. I'll share a couple

## RIGHT-BRAIN REFLECTION

What will it feel like to share your gift with the world? Reconnect with your big vision, values, and core message. Remember why you want to share this gift.

of high-level examples to illustrate the concepts and inspire you to develop your own personalized launch calendar and communications. Then, to give you a more strategic view of how to run your business, we'll talk about how you can map out multiple launches throughout the year for sustained success.

Keep in mind that launching is where the action heats up. You're putting a stake in the ground. You're making your idea real. You're putting yourself out there. Sure, it can feel scary and overwhelming if it's your first time (or, heck, even your fiftieth time!), whether it's a casual trial run that you invite a handful of friends to or it's the launch of your most ambitious product to date, announced to a worldwide following. No matter what, sharing your precious, wholehearted gifts with the world requires courage and the willingness to be vulnerable. So take a moment to acknowledge that. And remember, I'm here cheering you on!

## Don't Let Your Offers Collect Dust on the Shelf

Before we dive into launch plans, let's make a distinction between an ongoing marketing plan and a targeted launch campaign.

A plan for general marketing, or "getting the word out," outlines the ways you will reach out to your perfect customers on an ongoing basis. That may include using standard marketing media such as your website or blog, a store on Etsy, a newsletter, business cards, brochures, or flyers. It may also include regular networking, like attending professional events, doing speaking engagements, and using social media. I imagine you have some of these things already in place, or you may be working on them. You may not, however, be leveraging these media as effectively as you can (more on that in a bit).

Ongoing marketing — getting the word out — brings visibility to your brand and work, develops connections and relationships, and builds trust over the long-term, all of which are important to your success. If you want to sell something new, though, simply updating your website or brochure to include a description of the new offer, or doing a few announcements on social media, usually isn't enough. You need targeted promotions to drive traffic to your new product or service.

Unlike ongoing, regular marketing, a launch campaign highlights a specific offer made during a particular window of time to build buzz and create a sense of urgency.

For example, maybe you're announcing a new six-week program that starts next month. To communicate your offer, you may send direct, personal emails to a handful of previous clients and then follow up with individual phone calls. Or you may send a series of newsletter announcements to your list of subscribers, in addition to leading a free one-hour conference call where you provide a preview of some of what you'll teach in your new program. Or maybe to celebrate your latest line of paintings, you host an event at the gallery or coffee shop displaying your work and invite your followers to attend for a chance to win prizes and to take advantage of special pricing for pieces purchased that night.

## RIGHT-BRAIN REFLECTION

What are your goals for this launch? Take a moment to write down what success will look like for this particular launch. Is there a specific number of people you want to reach or grow your list by? Do you want to sell a certain number of items? Is there a specific dollar amount you want to earn in a certain amount of time? What do you want the energy of the launch to be like? How do you want people to respond?

Being clear about what success will look like for you will help you craft a launch plan that works.

A focused campaign generates awareness, invites engagement and action, and converts interest into sales in a specific time period. Otherwise your offers just sit there waiting for someone to find them. Here are two analogies to help illustrate this idea. Let's say you hang a beautiful piece of art on your family room wall. At first, you admire it every time you walk by. But after a while, you may not even notice it anymore because you're so used to seeing it there. It fades into the background. It's become so familiar that you forget it's there. So to direct attention to it, you put in some new overhead lighting. Or maybe every season you switch up the artwork to keep the look of your room fresh.

Also, consider your local grocery store. During the summer the endcaps spotlight sunscreen and picnic snacks, and at Thanksgiving the endcaps are piled high with cans of pumpkin pie filling and boxes of cornbread stuffing mix. Before you set foot in the store, you may have seen the products featured in their weekly circular, so you already know these items are on sale. The store has communicated the message in multiple media to build awareness. Any time of the year, you can probably find the sunblock or stuffing mix in their normal spots on the shelves. But by doing targeted marketing to promote these items and showcasing them prominently in season, the store makes it easier for you to buy them and they, in turn, increase their sales.

It's the same with your offers. It's great to list your products and services on your website, online store, or brochure. That's akin to having a regularly stocked item in its normal place on the shelf. But people who know they need it have to go find it, or it just collects dust. To increase sales or get a bump in new customers, draw attention to your offers, just like the grocery store does when it features the latest promotions on the endcaps. That's where targeted launches come in.

## Things to Consider for Your Launch

While I said there is no step-by-step formula to follow, there are some general guidelines that can frame your creative thinking about how you get the word out. I'll describe some of the typical phases in a launch and provide a few examples. But remember, your launch is unique to you and your circumstances.

You can use the Launch Plan play sheet to help you brainstorm how you will get the word out for each of these launch phases. Start from the bottom of the play sheet and work your way up.

### Generate Awareness with Tantalizing Teasers

Before your launch even begins, start planting some seeds to pique people's curiosity and get them excited about what's coming. Perhaps

**3**

Follow up, reminders and gentle nudges

Date range:

**2**

Open the doors and invite action

Date range:

**1**

Generate awareness with tantalizing teasers

Date range:

LAUNCH PLAN

you build anticipation via social media, saying something like: "I can't wait to tell you what I'm cooking up next for you" or "Stay tuned! Next week we've got some big announcements."

To appeal to the visual crowd, maybe you give peeks at some sketches, notes, prototypes, works in progress, or your planning process. A behind-the-scenes look at your production or preparation can involve people in what you're creating and help them appreciate what goes into your offer.

## Open the Doors and Invite Action

After you have primed your peeps with your tantalizing teasers and awareness-building activities, it'll be easier to hold their attention when you announce that your program is live or your new product is now available. They've been looking forward to hearing more details.

It can be helpful to host an event to officially open the doors and signify the launch. Just like in previous examples I mentioned, this might be an in-person celebration to exhibit your work or a hosted gathering where you demonstrate your artistic technique. Or maybe you lead a virtual session or an in-person class where people can experience you and your offering. Be creative. In what ways can your potential customers start engaging with you more deeply to learn more? What value can you provide now to give them a taste of how you can help them even more with your offer? In what ways do you truly shine when you're interacting with your perfect peeps? Use your reactions to these prompts to help you design what will work best for you and your customers.

When you open the doors, you'll also want to provide details about what you are offering, so that it's easy for people to sign up or buy. Look back at the love letter you crafted in chapter 5 for ways to communicate the benefits of the offer and to explain the details.

This is also a great time for your affiliates, creative cohorts, and strategic partners to spread the word and expand your reach. Make sure you've asked them a month or two ahead of time, or more, so they can schedule it on their own promotional calendars. Provide them with sample marketing copy and important dates, as well as their affiliate link so they will earn a commission when they sell something for you.

## Follow-ups, Reminders, and Gentle Nudges

After you've announced your offer, plan to follow up to keep your right people engaged, to address any concerns they have, and to remind them gracefully about what action you'd like them to take and by when.

Now, I imagine that the last thing you, a sensitive, heart-centered business owner, want is to come across as too pushy. But sometimes this means you may err on the side of not communicating enough. Unfortunately, though, you may miss out, and so will the people who really need your stuff but also need one more nudge. Anywhere from 30 to 50 percent of your sales can happen toward the end of a time-sensitive offer — up to the last minute. Not sending that final reminder could potentially mean leaving hundreds if not thousands of dollars in revenue on the table. Yikes! Sure, some people may unsubscribe, but they probably aren't your right people anyway. The more important thing is that your right people are able to benefit from the gifts you have to offer them, and that you give them opportunities to do just that.

A reminder may sound like: "Remember, you have only three more days to save" or "Don't forget: the doors close on this special offer on December 31, and I'd hate for you to miss out." I love it when I hear from people who say the last email came at just the right time, like a message from the universe telling them to take the leap.

Bottom line, make sure you schedule follow-ups and reminders. Make your follow-ups useful by including additional information that will help people decide if your offer is a good fit for them. That may entail answering some questions that have come from others and addressing concerns. It could be providing supplementary content that helps them deepen their experience with you or your product. Or it could be testimonials or photos of other customers who are already enjoying your product, which may inspire others to recognize how they can use it.

While it's helpful to have a general sense of the follow-up you plan to do, allow yourself to stay open and fluid. Pay attention to what resonates with people. What are they getting excited about? What are your raving fans sharing in social media? Those could be great quotes to include in your reminder messages. Listen to the questions that come in, and then write up a "frequently asked questions" follow-up message or blog post to clarify details and address concerns. By staying engaged with your audience, you'll continue to learn from them so that you can make your marketing and offer relevant and inspiring to them.

People love getting sneak peeks into the creative process. Build awareness of your upcoming launch by posting photos of works-in-progress on social media. Include tantalizing teasers like "Excited to share this new product with you next week!" in your photo captions.

# Launch Plan Examples

To help illustrate these ideas, on the following pages I've provided an example of a launch plan for a new program, including some sample key messages and timing details, followed by an example of a launch plan for a product. Remember, there is no cookie-cutter way to do a launch, so these examples are simply something your creative mind can respond to and shape into a plan that will work for you. Your plan may contain just a few line items, or it may be much more detailed than this, with specific messages for various target groups.

You may notice that the sample plans feel a bit left-brained in their structure. As a right-brainer, though, you'll find there are a few reasons why you can benefit from a systematic launch:

- Having a targeted launch campaign can help you track the effectiveness of your promotion and track the conversion from connection to customer. In other words, you can see how many people signed up to hear more about the upcoming offer, and then pinpoint what percentage of those leads actually end up buying your offer throughout your campaign.

- Depending on how big and complex your launch is, there can be a lot to do. Mapping out the details will actually give you peace of mind because the minutiae aren't swimming around in your head burning your mental energy. You'd rather spend that on your creative work, right?

- More than likely, you'll be enlisting your creative cohorts during the launch, and things will go much more smoothly if you have a plan. It's also more respectful of your cohorts when you provide clear instructions for how and when they can help promote you. Make it as easy as possible for them.

- When you have a documented launch plan, the next time you do a similar launch you can replicate and refine your process. Over time, you can create a workable system that you can repeat again and again. How's that for efficiency?

# Launch Plan Example for a Service or Program — a Six-Month Coaching Program

| AUDIENCE | SAMPLE MESSAGES | SAMPLE TIMING |
|---|---|---|
| **Generate awareness with tantalizing teasers:** | | |
| Whole email list | "It's coming/sneak peek/stay tuned." | 3–4 weeks out |
| Social media | "It's coming/sneak peek/stay tuned" and maybe include a photo. | 3–4 weeks out |
| Wait list or interested list (if you have one) | "Wanted to give you a heads-up that this new program is coming. As a VIP you get first dibs." | 3 weeks out |
| Whole email list | "It's here! Sign up for a free conference call to get a preview of what I'm teaching in this program and to find out more." Include any "I'm so excited" messages/quotes from responses by people on the interested list. | 2 weeks out |
| Free call list | "Reminder: free call is tomorrow." | Day before free call |
| **Open the doors and invite action:** | | |
| Free call list | Reminder: free call is today, in a few hours." | Day of free call |
| Social media | "Come join me on my free call." | Day of free call |
| Host the free call | Teach some topics from your program to give a sampling of the experience. Provide value to participants. Invite them to sign up for your program in order to work with you further. Include a special time-sensitive offer. | Day of free call |
| Free call list | Follow up after the call. Ask, "What takeaways did you get out of the experience?" (Note: This is also helpful market research/detective work for you.) | Day of free call |
| Preview call list | Replay link of free conference call and a link to your paid-program sign-up. | Day after free call |
| Whole email list | "Did you miss my free call? You can catch the recording (or you can join me for my encore)." Include a link to your sign-up page for the free call (or for encore call if you're doing one). | Day after free call |
| Free call list | Invitation to an encore call or a follow-up Q&A call. (An encore call is a repeat of the same teaching call, so people who missed the first one can participate live. In a follow-up Q&A call you answer questions sent in ahead of time, or asked live during the Q&A call, about the topic or details of the program.) | Few days after free call |
| Free call list | "Reminder: tomorrow is the encore call (or follow-up Q&A call)." | Day before follow-up call |
| Free call list | "Reminder: **today** is the encore call (or follow-up Q&A call)." | Day of follow-up call |
| Free call list | Include replay link of follow-up session; provide more info, buzz from previous calls, and so on. | Day after free call |
| **Follow-ups, reminders, gentle nudges:** | | |
| Free call list | Early-bird rate on paid program ends in five days (or other offer). | 5 days before early-bird ends |
| Social Media | Reminders about program, valuable tidbits of learning, important information, and so on. | Ongoing reminders |
| Whole email list | "Early-bird rate ends in five days," testimonials, or other key information. | 5 days before early-bird ends |
| Free call list | "Early-bird rate on paid program ends tomorrow." | Day before early-bird ends |
| Free call list | "Early-bird rate on paid program ends today." | Day early-bird ends |
| Whole email list | "Tomorrow is the last day to join the program"; include other tidbits, buzz, and so on. | 2nd-to-last day to join |
| Free call list | "Today is the last day to join the program"; include other tidbits, buzz, and so on. | Last day to join |

# Launch Plan Example for a Tangible Good or Other Product — a New, Limited-Edition Messenger Bag

| AUDIENCE | SAMPLE MESSAGES | SAMPLE TIMING |
|---|---|---|
| **Generate awareness with tantalizing teasers:** | | |
| Whole email list | "It's coming/sneak peek/stay tuned." Include photos of yourself in the studio or getting your product produced. | 3–4 weeks out |
| Social media and blog | "It's coming/sneak peek/stay tuned." Include photos of yourself in the studio or getting your product produced. | 3–4 weeks out |
| Wait list or interested list (if you have one) | "Wanted to give you a heads-up that my latest product is coming out soon. As a VIP you get first dibs, so mark your calendar." | 3 weeks out |
| Whole email list | Send a video of yourself sharing info about your product, with a stay-tuned date. | 2 weeks out |
| Social media and blog | Share your promo video. | 1–2 weeks out |
| **Open the doors and invite action:** | | |
| Wait list | "It's here! Special launch price through February 14. First twenty people to buy the product will get free shipping." | Day before public announcement |
| Whole email list | "It's here! Special launch price through February 14. First twenty people to buy the product will get free shipping" (if not all free-shipping spots were taken by your VIP wait list). Highlight enthusiastic responses from any of the early VIP buyers. | Day of announcement |
| Social media and blog | "It's here!" Link to promo page where customers can buy your product. | Day of announcement |
| **Follow-ups, reminders, gentle nudges:** | | |
| Wait list | "Special rate ends in three days. Only two more spots for free shipping." | February 11 |
| Social media | Send reminder about new product and special rates. | Ongoing reminders |
| Blog | "Special rate ends tomorrow. Here are some answers to questions we've been asked." | February 13 |
| Whole email list | "Today is the last day to get the special rate." | February 14 |
| Whole email list | Announce a contest: "The special rate has ended, but you still have a chance to win a prize. Send in a picture of yourself enjoying our product, and tell us why you love it. We'll announce winners next month." | February 16 |
| Blog | Send reminder about the contest deadline. Highlight some of the submissions you've already received. | March 6 |
| Whole email list | "Contest deadline is today." | March 16 |
| Whole email list and blog | "Contest winners announced." | March 17 |

Jumping headfirst into a launch before you build relationships is like going to a networking meeting and throwing your business card at everyone who walks in the door. You're likely to turn people off. But when you have a great relationship with your people, the launch can be much easier and more effective.

How can you start building trust now? How will people get to know you and experience you?

Contrary to what you may think, launching doesn't necessarily require having all your traditional ongoing marketing 100 percent complete and perfect (besides, it will never be perfect!). For example, I see so many right-brain entrepreneurs get stuck, spending months designing and fine-tuning their main website before they feel like they can launch. They spend all this time writing the perfect copy to describe every single idea they've ever had for a product or service. While they're focused on the minutiae, no moola is flowing in. And they're wondering why they're frustrated with their business.

You can launch a very specific campaign with focused marketing media and messages to simply test an offer. You don't need to have your entire brand presence ready first. In fact, engaging customers with the product or service will help you refine the offer and make more compelling copy by incorporating what you learn about how these customers benefited.

## Infrastructure Essentials

If this is your first launch, keep your process and infrastructure to a bare minimum. That way you're not overinvesting. Instead of increasing your expenses early on, focus on bringing moola in.

The basic things to have in place are a way for people to pay you (see chapter 7 for ideas) and a way for you to communicate with your potential customers and paying customers (a simple email marketing service like MailChimp or Constant Contact will do). Your process may be manual at first, and that's probably okay if it's a manageable volume. Besides, having your hands in the process will help you understand what goes into fulfilling a sale and communicating with your customers. We'll explore setting up your infrastructure and your Smooth Sailing Systems in chapter 9.

## Mapping Out Your Launches for the Year

Now that you have a sense of what goes into a single launch, let's take it a step further and explore how you can map out launches that will take place throughout the year to create sustained success.

Once you have various offers in place, it's easier to start thinking strategically about how you can promote them throughout the year(s), and how the "leaves" will add up to the income listed on your flower.

A giant wall calendar provides ample space to plan out your launches. During my Right-Brain Business Plan workshop hosted by creativeLIVE, I helped image consultant and wardrobe stylist Caitlin Colling map out her key milestones and moola-making opportunities for the year. Photo © Rebecca Stumpf.

I like to do a high-level map of the whole year using my sticky-note project plan. That gives me the lay of the land. I typically do two larger-scale launches per year, usually in the first and third quarters, and smaller-scale launches in the second and fourth quarters. That way I have just one main launch per quarter. I may be doing other offers in the other months, but most of my energy and resources are focused on those quarterly launches.

You can do an exercise that will acquaint you with this, using the Quarterly Moola Goals illustrated play sheet to map out your launches and estimated earnings by quarter. In the top row write out what you want to accomplish per quarter (such as "Fill twenty seats in my six-month program" or "Sell thirty commissioned paintings" or "Build my list to ten thousand subscribers." Next, list your key launch(es) by month and include the estimated income for each month in the box with the dollar sign. Add up the total moola goal for each quarter, and then add up the total for all quarters to calculate your moola goal for the year. You can also work backward from the moola goal for the year and allocate the total across the quarters based on the estimated scale of your launches.

Once I have broad brushstrokes for the year, I focus on the current quarter. For launches in that quarter that require specific schedules or project plans, I dive into that next level of detail in Word or Excel (or on Google Docs if I need to share them in real time with other team members). The great thing about documenting the launch process as you go is that you'll have your own blueprint for the next time around. See chapter 9 for more tips on documenting procedures and creating your Smooth Sailing Systems.

Here are a few different ways to approach planning out your launches.

# QUARTERLY MOOLA GOALS

| QUARTER 1 GOALS: | QUARTER 2 GOALS: | QUARTER 3 GOALS: | QUARTER 4 GOALS: |
|---|---|---|---|
| January | April | July | October |
| $ | $ | $ | $ |
| February | May | August | November |
| $ | $ | $ | $ |
| March | June | September | December |
| $ | $ | $ | $ |

Q1 Moola Goal + Q2 Moola Goal + Q3 Moola Goal + Q4 Moola Goal =

TOTAL: 

Moola Goal for the Year

## Seasonal Planning Play Sheet

You can use the illustrated Seasonal Planning play sheet to brainstorm ways to align certain launches or promotions with certain times of the year, such as holidays and special occasions, or with seasonal interest. List launch ideas per season and, if you can, include rough timelines and details about each special offer. For example, in the winter section you might write, "Holiday sale December 1–7! All card sets and journals 20 percent off." Here are some seasonal themes to spur your own creative thinking:

- Beginning of the year — focus on goal-setting.
- Tax time in April — focus on finances.
- Spring — focus on spring cleaning.
- Mother's Day and Father's Day — focus on parenting, parenthood, or families.
- Graduation season — focus on transitions and next steps.
- Valentine's Day — focus on romance, relationships, self-love.
- Fourth of July — focus on freedom and independence.
- Thanksgiving — focus on gratitude.
- Fall — focus on back-to-school.
- Summer — highlight fun, vacation, freedom, playfulness, kids out of school, or being outside.
- Winter — highlight the holidays, colder weather, the gift-giving season, people being less physically active, or end-of-year closure and celebration.

Since other businesses, too, may be piggybacking on holidays and seasons, you can zig when they zag by launching your offer during a less "crowded" time that still makes sense for your customers.

What products or services align nicely with some of the topics I've listed here? How can your offer highlight the benefits and be timely for your perfect customers?

What season is generally slower for your business? Are there weeks or months when you know you'll need to focus on development but will still want to bring in cash? That could be a great time to run a sale

# Seasonal planning

SPRING

SUMMER

WINTER

FALL

on existing products or services. The nice thing is that the work has already been developed, so the launch effort amounts to simply creating and delivering your marketing messages.

## Anticipate What Your Customers Need Next

Another way to look at mapping out your launches for the year (and years to come) is to anticipate the natural cycles in your customers' lives or growth journeys. Are there things they would want or need after their first purchase from you? Where do you see them going next? What themes are you hearing within your community of fans and customers? What do clients ask about after they make their first purchases? Those are clues to the offers you can consider mapping out over the course of the year and beyond.

If you're a service provider, your initial work may take your clients to a new level, after which they'll be ready for the next. For example, a holistic health practitioner may have a two-day cleanse for a juicing newbie. If the client wants to go further, she may do a five-day cleanse the next month and then require some nutritional counseling to go back to her normal diet. Or a wedding photographer may notice that his clients are now becoming expectant moms and dads who may be interested in pregnancy portraits or photo shoots with their growing families.

If you sell products, consider whether they'll need, for example, refills for the notebook they buy from you. Or perhaps additional charms for their handmade necklace? An upgrade from the basic product to the one with the latest features? Different color accessories for the seasons? A companion piece that matches the item they bought?

Whether you provide a service or sell products, anticipating your customer's next needs will help you map out your future offers.

## Take a Breather

When you're mapping out the seasons and quarters, also plan time for taking some breaks. As an eager right-brained creative, you may find it easy to become overzealous about getting all your ideas out there. But realistically, you're going to want some breathers in between your promotions. Back-to-back launches are just not sustainable. With overlapping launches, not only do you have a lot to manage all at once, but you also run the risk of confusing or inundating your people.

Make sure you have enough time in between launches to develop products and content, set everything up for the launch, run the launch, and still allow recovery time for yourself and your people. My guess is, you probably don't want to bombard them nonstop with things to buy. Remember, it's a relationship that you're building, so think, too, about the ongoing value or support you can provide when you're not selling anything directly.

Also, keep in mind that your new launches can build on earlier ones. For example, a promotional launch for a free offer designed to build buzz and exposure can be followed up shortly afterward with a launch of a more extensive paid program or product related to what they just had a taste of.

## LEFT-BRAIN CHILL PILL

Build in downtime as part of your launch plan. You'll need time to decompress afterward. After a big event, I sometimes experience a bit of depression and withdrawal, and I know that's part of my creative process. Rather than continue to push myself, I let myself have days where I just stay in bed and hide under the covers.

## Not All Launches Are Equal

In chapter 5 we talked about packaging your gifts and crafting your offers. Not every launch will be for a big fancy gift. Some may be for simple brown-paper packages tied up with string, and those can be light-touch and low-key. A light launch may amount to a handful of personal invitations to test out a new workshop, or a onetime announcement via email sent to key wholesalers who order your products, plus a follow-up phone call.

If you're doing the big launch of a new flagship product or signature system that will be your main moola-maker for the quarter or even the year, you'll benefit from a more robust, detailed launch plan. For example, for one of my big annual virtual events, my launch plan typically has more than a hundred line items, and I sometimes send multiple messages per day to each of several specific audiences. For example, during the course of a day I may send a reminder that the free session starts in one hour, a separate message with the replay link after the session is over, and a reminder message about a group coaching call to people who upgraded to the paid coaching package.

The point here is to avoid overkill and not treat every single launch you do with the same effort. It's just not sustainable.

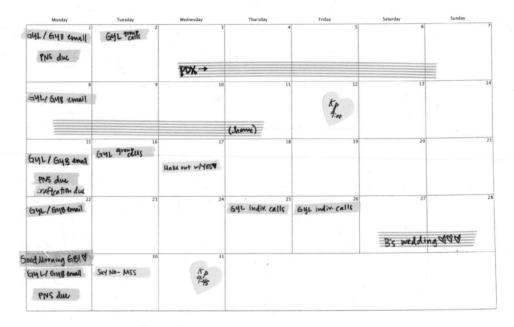

Spice up your launch plan calendar with colorful washi tape, just like life and business coach Tiffany Han does to keep track of key dates.

## Launch, Then Create

The book you now hold in your hands is an example of "launch, then create." You see, I didn't have a final, fully designed and edited book before the publisher bought rights to the material or before we launched it. I wrote the bulk of it after we had set a publication date and signed a contract. Of course, it wasn't like I was starting completely from scratch. I had other pieces to pull from. But the point is that I didn't have to finish writing the book before the publisher announced a publication date so bookstores could be ready to sell it.

A publicized launch date initiates focused action. And when you already have money on the table from folks who are expecting you to deliver — well, you've just raised the stakes and by golly you'll get something done.

Launch, then create, is way more effective than waiting (and waiting, and waiting) for the muse to strike, or than revising your product for the hundredth time to make sure it is utterly perfect before ever telling a soul about it. It still won't be perfect, so stop kidding yourself and stop holding back your gifts from the people who need your help now.

If launch, then create, scares you because you're afraid you won't finish in time, or that you're not ready, realize that you've been creating all along if you've been engaging with your ideas, journaling about them, and talking about them with close friends. Most likely, you're not starting from scratch, so trust that you have experience and lots of rough drafts to draw from. Coach Tiffany Han says,

> I've found that the launch-then-create method is the only one that works for me. I'm a class-A procrastinator, so unless I'm working on a hard deadline, nothing gets done, ever. Rather than hating this about myself and constantly trying to change it, I've learned to embrace it and accept that it's just part of how I work. I love beta-testing products and think it's a really important part of the product creation process, but who says you can't still earn a little moola in the process? I've always been up front with my customers when they're part of a beta program, and I use it to their advantage: by giving me feedback as we go, they get what they need most from the product or program or course. And I, in turn, get real-time, dynamic market research about what my peeps need. It's a win-win.

Here are some examples of what launch, then create, looks like:

- If you're an artist or crafter, register for a table at an art show or street fair. The hard deadline for when you must show up and fill your booth with your wares will get you moving.
- If you're a photographer, put a deposit down on a studio that you'll rent for an afternoon. Then publicize your upcoming portrait party and offer a special rate for the first ten people who sign up.
- If you're a coach, announce the date of your workshop even before you've fully finished the content.
- If you're a maker, start accepting preorders on your next product.

This is not about being irresponsible or unprofessional or doing a half-assed job. That's not you. You probably put your whole heart into your work and overdeliver anyway. What this is about is creating real accountability so that you finally get your offer out there. It would be a disservice for you to keep your gifts from those who need them right now. You can always improve your product over time. But by putting something out there now, you get both feedback and income.

A launch is another opportunity for learning. You get to learn what works and what doesn't, what messages resonate with your fans and followers and turn them into paying customers, what price points appeal to people, and more. Remember the "fertilizer" I talked about in the Entrepreneurial Ecosystem discussion? When a launch doesn't go as well as planned, it may feel crappy at first but you can grow from there.

## ACTION ACCELERATOR

Draft the love letter first. Describing your product's benefits and features will help you refine what you're creating and clarify what you want to accomplish. What will you test when you launch, then create? It depends on what you want to find out. You can test the price point. Or test the offer: Is this what people want? Do they buy it? What questions do they ask? Give some of it away for free or at low cost just to get people engaged with your work. Then get feedback, ideas, testimonials, or photographs of happy customers using your product or of yourself delivering your service.

When I first tried to launch my group mentorship program, only one person signed up. Poo. After feeling sorry for myself for a few months, I picked myself up, made adjustments to the packaging and pricing based on feedback, and relaunched the program successfully. Stay open and evolve your next offer, and launch from there. Remember, building your business is a creative process.

## Recap of Activities

- Develop your launch plan.
- Launch, then create.
- Map out your launches for the year using the Seasonal Planning play sheet.

 **LEFT-BRAIN CHECKLIST**

Your left brain appreciates keeping track of the steps you've taken toward your sustained success.

- ❑ I have been deepening my relationships with my perfect customers.
- ❑ I have been deepening relationships with my key supporters and influencers.
- ❑ I have a launch plan in place for my upcoming offer. I've identified my key messages, audience, and timing.
- ❑ I have the basic infrastructure I need to run the launch.
- ❑ I have communicated all the important information to the key supporters who are helping me with my launch.
- ❑ I know what I'm testing in my launch and what a successful launch means for this offer.
- ❑ I have built in time to decompress after my launch.
- ❑ I have mapped out my launches for the next quarter or year.

# 7 Making More Moola

## Optimize Opportunities for Ongoing Earning

As a right-brain entrepreneur, you're passionate about your work. You're in business to make a difference. And — let's cut straight to the chase — you're in business to make money, too, right?

Let's take a moment to look back at your Business Flower from the Entrepreneurial Ecosystem. How are you feeling about reaching your moola goal now? In chapter 5 we explored ways for you to package your gifts and craft your offers so that you'll have the right leaves on your flower stem. And in chapter 6 we talked about how to launch your products and service offerings into the world. Those two essential business activities are key to making more moola.

In this chapter we'll dive into more detail about moola-making to help you optimize opportunities for ongoing earning. We'll cover three basic ways to make more moola in your business, why it's important to track your moola, and ideas for multiple moola-making methods.

We'll also tap into your right-brain creativity to explore what you want from your moola. It's not really about the number; it's about what your money can make possible for your life and your business.

## Three Basic Paths to Making More Moola

While many of us get tied up in knots racking our brains for all the different ways we can make more money, it actually doesn't need to be so complicated. According to marketing expert Jay Abraham in his book *Getting Everything You Can Out of All You've Got*, there are just three paths to making more money (my interpretation is in brackets):

- Increase the number of clients [in other words, increase the number of your sales to new customers].
- Increase the average size of the sale per client [in other words, increase your prices].
- Increase the number of times clients return and buy again [in other words, increase the frequency of your sales to existing customers].

That's pretty straightforward, right?

So, rather than spinning your wheels while deciding how to make more moola, you can always return to these three paths at any given time and ask yourself which one will serve you best.

Depending on where you are in your business, just starting out or well-established but looking for ways to grow, one path may make more sense than the others. Let's talk about each path so you can decide which one to follow right now.

### Increasing the Number of Your Sales to New Customers

To increase your income, gaining new customers can be a great place to start if you're new to business or you're growing a new arm of your business. With this strategy, you expand your reach outside your normal channels so you can connect with a larger audience. I've highlighted a handful of ideas here for broadening your base of potential customers.

You can also return to chapter 4 of this book for additional suggestions, and you can check out chapter 4 of *The Right-Brain Business Plan.*

Some ways to expand your reach:

- Build your email and social media lists.
- Be interviewed on a radio or TV show, a popular podcast, or a telesummit or video summit.
- Be a guest speaker at an event.
- Do guest blog posts on sites that your perfect customers visit.
- Host a free in-person event that gives people a taste of your work.
- Host a virtual event where you give free information or interview guest experts. Audience members register to get access to the event plus a subscription to your newsletter.
- Offer a free gift to those who add their names to your email marketing list.
- Host a contest or a give-away related to your work.

> ## TIP
>
> Depending on your business land-scape, sometimes lowering your price points (even temporarily) can help you get more customers and, in essence, bring in more money as a result of increased volume. This could be something to play with if you've been struggling for a while to convert followers or subscribers into actual paying customers.

## Increasing Your Prices

Raising your prices is a good path to take if you have folks willing to pay the higher prices. And you really won't know if they are until you test it!

An indicator that it's time to increase your price on something is that you sell out of it rather quickly. If you notice your competitors are charging more for a similar product and the market is bearing it, consider raising your prices too. Customers may even say you should charge more, so by all means listen to them! That's great feedback on the perceived value they're receiving. Raising your prices can also elevate your prestige and position in the marketplace, because people expect to pay more for higher quality.

If you want to service fewer customers, ones who are willing to pay a premium, this can be a good model for you. Take into account, though, that you'll probably have a longer sales cycle for the higher investment — meaning, more time may elapse between your initial connection and their actual purchase. With the higher price tag you'll also need to go deeper with your clients or provide even more value than you would if you were serving more people. Think about how you can enhance the experience when you raise your prices. Is there a special bonus or a more advanced

## PRICING

 I wish I could tell you there's a magic formula for pricing. But really it depends on what you're selling and who your market is. There are two simple schools of thought. One is a bottom-up approach that takes into account your costs and adds a markup sufficient to create a profit. In the top-down approach, you determine the highest price your customers are willing to pay, based on perceived value, and charge that.

You won't know if the price is right until you test it. If you offer a product for, let's say, a hundred dollars, does someone actually give you that amount in exchange for it? Do more or fewer people purchase it than you anticipated? Was it like pulling teeth to make the sale, or were the orders flying in? Of course there are other factors, like your marketing strategies, that influence whether people buy, but certainly price is something to pay attention to.

If you have a line of products and services, look at the prices of your various offers and how they relate to each other. Is there a natural progression that makes sense as you go up the price list? Is there added value or exclusivity that comes with the higher price tags?

As you can see, pricing is part art and part science. To set a price, you find the intersection of what you feel comfortable charging and what your customers are willing to pay. Even if you land on a price that works, keep in mind that the business landscape changes, customer needs evolve, and your own interests, resources, or costs may shift. It's important to keep tabs on what's working and to be nimble and adaptable.

program you can offer? Can you use higher-quality raw materials?

Sometimes folks increase their prices by just a tad, say, ten dollars an hour or 5 percent. However, if you're going to raise your prices, make the increase more significant to really signal a change. Be confident in the value you provide, and let your rates reflect that.

> ## RIGHT-BRAIN BOOSTER
> For a prosperity pick-me-up, listen to Karen Drucker's inspiring tune "Prosperity Chant" on her *Songs of the Spirit II* album (www.karendrucker .com/store/songs-of-the-spirit-2/). Her spiritual song will get you grooving to the rhythm of good fortune and abundance in no time.

## Increasing the Frequency of Your Sales to Existing Customers

If you've been in business for a while, focusing on repeat customers is a great way to maximize your current client base. You've already invested time and resources to transform these connections into paying clients, so make the most of your existing relationships. Chances are your clients have been growing along with you and their needs have evolved. Find more ways to meet their new needs. What new value-added resources, content, materials, products, or bonuses can you provide that would take them to the next level or enhance their lives in new ways?

Ask yourself: What's next in your relationship with your customers? What do you hear them asking for? Where can you see them going next (even if they don't quite see it yet themselves)? Pay attention to what you hear in conversations and to what they share online. This is where your right-brain superpowers — intuition, connection, empathy, and your knack for listening, as well as your ability to see patterns and the big picture — will come in handy.

One of the best ways to find out what else you can offer them is to ask them. Simply ask your individual clients what they might like next from you. Offer new packages to meet their specific needs, or make special offers to your favorite customers and see how they respond. You can send out a survey to all your past and current clients with questions about what they need help with, what their most pressing challenges are, or what they would love to see from you. You could invite your customers to an open conference call or town-hall-style meeting and generate discussion to see what's on their minds. You could have office hours and be available to answer questions and connect with customers. You could ask a question in your newsletter and see what type of responses you get.

## ACTION ACCELERATOR

Want a challenge? What can you sell today (yes, TODAY!) to bring in ten dollars, a hundred dollars, or even a thousand dollars? Usually it's the simplest offer you already have or something you've been doing for a while. For example, you could run a sale on existing goods or services, or bundle items together and sell them for a special rate, or personally extend an invitation to a few friends or colleagues you would love to work with (sometimes all you have to do is ask!).

In chapter 6 we touched on the natural cycle in your customers' lives, so you can refer back to that section for more ideas or examples.

Which path will you try? Which one feels like your fastest path to cash right now?

Shake your moola-maker and sell something (even if it's something in your personal life) to help get the energy and abundance flowing right now. Get creative! Here are just a few ideas to spark your money magnetism:

- Run a sale on existing products. (This is a great go-to for a boost in cash flow.)
- Run a clearance sale on old inventory.
- Offer a VIP coaching session to your list. (All it takes is one person signing up for a high-end package.)
- Extend a special invitation to a few friends or colleagues. (When I was getting my first coaching clients, I approached people I wanted to work with and said, "Hey I'd really love to work with you, and here's how I think I can help you. I'm offering this special rate. Would you be my client?" And lo and behold, some said yes!)
- Promote a fellow cohort's products or services through his affiliate program and earn a commission from the sales you make. (I've made anywhere from tens of dollars to thousands of dollars in a day simply as an affiliate of other people's products.)

- Sell your used books. (When I was moving to a new house, I traded some books back to Amazon. I made more than a hundred dollars, and I got rid of clutter. Score!)
- Have a garage sale.
- Auction equipment or raw materials you don't use anymore on eBay.

## Diversifying Your Moola-Making Methods

A more advanced way to earn more money is to diversify your moola-making methods. This can help you get new customers because your new offers may target a new type of customer in your market. It can also help you sell more to existing customers if you're offering something else they need. And in some ways it can help you increase your prices for your one-to-one services or handmade, money-for-time products (more on that in a bit).

I briefly mentioned the Multiple Moola-Making Methods Map in chapter 5, when you were working on packaging your gifts and crafting your offers. Let's dive into this concept more deeply now that we're looking at the moola side of things. If you're still working on your foundational products and services, look at this section as an option you can pursue later as part of a longer-term strategy. If you already have your base offerings up and running smoothly, start exploring how you can diversify.

The Multiple Moola-Making Methods Map illustrates how having various income streams can create increased profits from leveraging your time and resources more effectively. Rather than confining yourself to a money-for-time model, you can make more moola and help more people in the same or even less amount of time. If you're a service provider, consider turning some of your individual services into group offerings or into products. You can use the Multiple Moola-Making Methods Map to help you identify where you are right now with your offers and to brainstorm future ways you can maximize money coming in.

# Multiple Moola-Making Methods Map

## Services

| $ FOR TIME | LEVERAGED | "PASSIVE" $ |
|---|---|---|
| 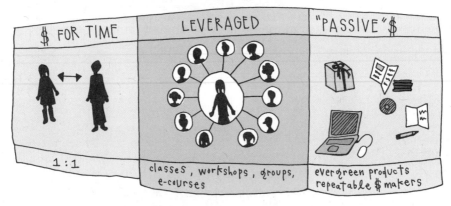 | | |
| 1:1 | classes, workshops, groups, e-courses | evergreen products repeatable $ makers |

## PRODUCTS

| $ FOR ITEM | LEVERAGED | "PASSIVE" $ |
|---|---|---|
|  | | |
| 1:1 | classes, workshops, groups, e-courses | production support, patterns, tutorials, licensing artwork, mass produce, agent or sales rep |

It's a good idea to start with what you know, and for most service providers this means working with individual clients. Then you realize you can help more people at once by packaging your process into a workshop, so you start leading people through the process in a group. Then as your workshops gain momentum, you can turn the workshop into a book or product that people can download as a self-study program.

To see how this could play out numberwise, here is a sample of a simplified Multiple Moola-Making Methods Map just for discussion purposes.

Meet Jane, who is a holistic health consultant. Let's use a simple round number and say that her hourly rate for individual client sessions is $100. So, the first column, which is money for time, shows that one hour spent with one client yields $100. If Jane has ten individual clients, and she meets with each of them once a month, she makes $1,000 per month for ten hours of her time.

The second column, which is leveraged moola-making, shows that Jane has expanded her services to include one-hour group sessions with ten people in each group at $40 each. And every time she runs a full session, she gets $400 for that hour of work (rather than $100 for an hour with an individual client). If she holds five group sessions each month, she can make $2,000 per month for five hours of her time. She earns twice as much as in the individual-client scenario, in half the time.

The third column, which is passive income, shows that Jane has created a six-module Better Eating, Better You, home-study course that is delivered via email. Let's say she spent ten hours creating the course and she sells it for $100. If she sells twenty copies in the first month, she earns $2,000 for that initial ten-hour investment in content development (this is on top of the income she continues to make from working with her individual clients and group sessions). What makes this supplemental income "passive" is that, with merely some additional administration and marketing time, she can conceivably continue to make $2,000 a month — which would total $24,000 at the end of the year — for that initial ten hours of work. This example shows how you can earn the same amount of money, or more, for less time.

# The Evolution of the Multiple Moola-Making Methods Map

When you've created a strong foundation for the business, you can bring in more income by creating multiple moola-making methods. If your company is mostly a service business, see where you can turn your expertise or content into products. If you create products, diversify by also providing services.

| | Moola for Time (One-Person Operation) | Leveraged Moola-Making | "Passive" Moola-Making: Steady Earning over the Long-Term (Expanding Your Enterprise) |
|---|---|---|---|
| **Services: Progression of Productizing Your Service** | • Offer one-to-one sessions with clients.<br>• Set an hourly rate.<br>• Develop time-based projects.<br>• Create bundled packages of sessions or services.<br>• Charge more for VIP individual sessions. | • Offer in-person classes and workshops.<br>• Group sessions maximize your time and are more cost-effective for participants.<br>• Offer online courses.<br>• Offer teleclasses.<br>• Offer webinars.<br>• Offer telesummits or video summits, where you invite guest speakers; then turn the event into an info product.<br>• Offer a train-the-trainer or certification program.<br>• Undertake joint ventures. | • Make evergreen products and repeatable moola-makers.<br>• Offer information products — downloadable PDFs, videos, and MP3s with content and/or instructions.<br>• License your intellectual property and sell the rights to others, who will use your proprietary content or deliver your programs.<br>• Have a subscription, membership, or monthly-fee business model for existing content, creating stable, steady income online<br>• Create an affiliate program. |
| **Products: Progression of Creating Services out of Your Products** | • Sell handmade items.<br>• Offer bundles of products for a special price.<br>• Offer commissioned work — charge a premium for custom projects. | • Offer private or semiprivate classes.<br>• Offer workshops.<br>• Sell patterns.<br>• Sell tutorials.<br>• Go into joint ventures. | • License your work — sell rights to others who will use your designs, illustrations, and patterns.<br>• Get an agent to help you.<br>• Mass-produce items.<br>• Hire someone to do production for you.<br>• Offer an affiliate program. |

| | Moola for Time (One-Person Operation) | Leveraged Moola-Making | "Passive" Moola-Making: Steady Earning over the Long-Term (Expanding Your Enterprise) |
|---|---|---|---|
| Considerations | • Start with what you know (this is usually the entry point).<br>• Learn and get ideas from working directly with your customers and from indirect customer contact/feedback; test things out, see what works, and use this data to maximize future moola-making methods.<br>• Learn skills.<br>• Get more experience; cut your teeth.<br>• Build relationships and your reputation.<br>• This is an easier place to start from, because you don't need much infrastructure. It's probably the fastest path to cash.<br>• Growing your business by adding leveraged and passive income doesn't mean that you need to give up one-to-one offers. When your business is better established, you can charge premium prices for money-for-time exchanges, because VIP customers have exclusive access to you or your work. | • Get more feedback.<br>• See themes show up in real time in groups.<br>• You still charge money for time, but you can make more money in the same amount of time.<br>• Record classes or events and turn the result into a passive-income product.<br>• Start building your tribe/community as you gather groups of your right peeps together. Gain momentum.<br>• Collect testimonials.<br>• If you're doing something in person, get photos of yourself leading groups.<br>• As you branch out into leveraged moola-making methods, you most likely will need to develop some new skills or will need to build your team. You can't expect to automatically know how to do everything, so factor in the learning curve. | • It's hard to jump directly here without having a tribe. Usually you need to have a following or a list of people to sell the products to.<br>• If you're an artist or other maker, perhaps build up your portfolio and get your work licensed.<br>• Expand your reach.<br>• Help more people at once.<br>• It takes more time up front to build income this way, so you might not amass an income right away.<br>• This category requires more technical infrastructure and usually a team or some type of administrative support. |

If you create handmade items, consider augmenting your product sales with service offerings such as teaching classes or hosting retreats. For example, artist Amy Crawley makes ornaments and sculptures out of polymer clay. At art shows, people began asking her how to work with polymer clay, so in addition to selling her artwork Amy branched out and began teaching classes. She offers private individual and small-group sessions and leads other classes at venues such as museums and art schools. As part of Amy's longer-term Right-Brain Business Plan, she'd like to offer online art classes as well, which will include videos and tutorials. An additional way for crafters and artists like Amy to maximize moola-making and create passive income could be to mass-produce items, license original artwork, or have an agent or rep sell on their behalf.

Ho'omalamalama Brown explores how her fitness and creativity business can evolve from just offering money-for-time services to eventually offering products and more.

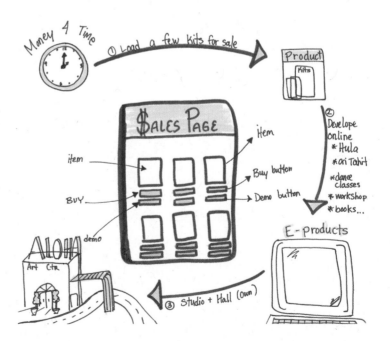

Sharon Tessandori is a life coach and the owner of Barefoot Works yoga studio in Lexington, Kentucky. After she left her full-time salaried job, Sharon taught group yoga classes anywhere she could during her first two years in business. Then she took the leap in 2006 and opened up a yoga studio. Sharon describes how she's expanded her moola-making methods over the years:

Ten months after opening my yoga studio, I led my first yoga retreat, a weeklong international yoga retreat in Tulum, Mexico. Five months after that, I led my first two-hundred-hour yoga-teacher training. It was the first training of this nature in Lexington. I continued focusing on retreats and yoga-teacher trainings because I utterly loved them and they brought in much more revenue than group classes. I've led sold-out retreats and trainings by the Atlantic Ocean, Pacific Ocean, and Caribbean Sea.

Now Sharon is expanding into life coaching with a yoga-minded spin. As a new mom, she has discovered that this additional moola-making method helps her continue to pursue her passions with the necessary flexibility in location and schedule.

## Knowing Your Numbers

If your approach to dealing with your numbers is to bury your head in the sand, you're probably inflicting undue stress on yourself. Knowing what's going on in your business is actually empowering. You have the information you need in order to see any gaps, and you can make choices about what you can do to hit your target numbers. Do you need to increase prices? Cut down on expenses? Make more offers to existing customers?

In *The Right-Brain Business Plan* book, I provided a simple spreadsheet called Rid the Red, Grow the Green, which you can download here:

www.rightbrainbusinessplan.com/rbbiz. Use this to track your current moola-in and moola-out by month and make estimates for the remainder of the year. The first time you fill it out may feel like a stab in the dark, but as you start to track your income and expenses it will get easier.

Here are some basic numbers to track regularly:

- How much moola did you bring in this week?
- How much moola did you spend this week?
- What's your profit for this week? Or this month?
- How much moola do you want to bring in by the end of the month? And what will it take to make that happen? Be as specific as you can (what you must sell at what price to how many people).
- On a scale of one to ten, how receptive to abundance are you feeling (one being not at all, and ten being totally ready)? If your score isn't where you'd like it to be, what can you do to move the needle?

Meditation teacher Bindi Shah created affirmations to remind her about the value she provides to her clients. As a result of this practice, she's stayed on top of her numbers. And she's pleased to see her numbers are increasing.

I look at these numbers weekly, and when I'm in the middle of a launch I may even look at them daily. I get an in-the-moment read of moola-in and moola-out by using GoDaddy Bookkeeping software, which tracks my business bank accounts. I use the reporting function in my e-commerce system to see how many sales I've made and how many automated payments I am expecting. And every month when I receive my reconciled accounts in Quickbooks from my bookkeeper, I review my profit-and-loss statement for the previous month and the year to date.

As your business starts to grow and you have more offerings, you'll also find it helpful to pay attention to more detailed data, such as:

- How many sign-ups do you get per launch, and how many sales?
- When do more sales happen? Do they happen at the beginning of a launch or at the end? After you make certain announcements or offer particular promotions?
- What are your bestselling products? What price range are they in?
- What are your most profitable products? Are they things you want to keep selling more of? How many of those do you need to sell to reach your moola goal?
- How many upgrades did you sell? What prompted the upgrade? Was it a special or a particular invitation or marketing message?
- Who are your repeat customers? Are there certain customers who consistently spend more? How can you continue to serve them and add value to their experience?
- In which months did you make more sales? What was different for you in those months? Did you sell more of one thing? Did you sell higher-priced items? Did you land a big project or commission? Is any of it easily repeatable? How can you use that to

## TIP

If you feel like you're working yourself to the bone, and you aren't reaching the earnings you want, go through the list of your current moola-making methods and guesstimate how much time you spend on each. Identify which ones are more profitable versus which ones are costing you money or missed opportunities. If you were to make the majority of your money in one to three key areas, which would they be? Are you willing to let the other ones go or at least look at repackaging them to make them more profitable?

inform your overall launch plan for the year and when you factor in the development of your moola-later projects?

## RIGHT-BRAIN ENTREPRENEUR SPOTLIGHT

A story about Elle Roberts, cofounder of the Artful Business Conference, is a great example of how knowing your numbers helps you make your ideas real.

When I first decided I wanted to run the Artful Business Conference, I sat down and wrote a budget. Seeing the numbers [$50,000 in expenses] almost put an end to everything. I was a single mom trying to make a new creative business work, and I had bills to pay and $400 in my bank account. The $50,000 made my heart stop. For a few months I ignored the dollars. If I looked at them, I felt physically ill.

I knew getting comfortable with the numbers was something I needed to do. I can't even really say why, but I wrote "$50,000" on Post-its, and stuck them all over my house. There was "$50,000" written on notes on my fridge and my bathroom mirror, on my car steering wheel and my laptop. They were everywhere. After a while, it stopped being so scary and started being just another number.

Getting comfortable with the number helped Elle focus on what she needed to do to make the event happen. She figured out how many tickets she had sell at what price, she sold sponsorships, and she got creative and sold live-streamed virtual seats. And in September 2012 she successfully hosted the first-ever Artful Business Conference, in Brisbane, Australia.

## Moola Now versus Moola Later

Creative entrepreneurs can get so enamored by their never-ending flow of bright ideas that they can sometimes lose sight of the here and now.

# RIGHT-BRAIN ENTREPRENEUR SPOTLIGHT

A veteran business owner for more than thirty years, Susan Miller grew her private therapy practice from the early days of seeing clients in her living room to later leading a team of administrative staff and contract therapists in an eighteen-hundred-square-foot office and bringing in five figures a month. At that point she realized she had grown too fast. And when both her therapists left, she experienced a challenging financial loss. In 2012 she took a long, hard look at her numbers and made some tough decisions to get her business financially healthy again.

Given that her rent was a huge, recurring expense, Susan approached her landlord and explained her situation. He not only offered to give her a $450 break for several months, but he also helped her advertise for someone to rent part of her space. She negotiated contracts with her new therapists as well, to take into account monthly overhead expenses. And by switching to more affordable options for her phone service, billing software, and voicemail; scaling back her office space; and consolidating some jobs, Susan was able to cut her expenses by $3,000 a month.

If your expenses are killing your profits, be inspired by Susan's tenacity and her willingness to dig into the numbers. Now her business is thriving again, and she's even expanding it to include a creative coaching and workshop arm that helps express her latest passions.

To keep her counseling and coaching businesses healthy, Susan Miller had to take a long, hard look at how she organized her team and managed her moola.

They're so busy developing the next big thing that they overlook ways to bring in money right now, and then wonder why they're stressed out about unpaid bills.

Sometimes, the best thing to do for yourself and your business is to work on getting moola in *now* in the easiest and quickest way possible. That may mean doing work for a while that isn't your number one love. In your own creative business you may have a moola-now "day job" that helps keep you afloat, and a moola-later "side job" that is less proven but sexier and more fun. That's okay. As your own boss you can ensure that your day job is not soul-sucking, and that you are allowing time to test and grow the side job. Also, continue to look at the numbers to be sure you're indeed making an overall profit; otherwise you're working your butt off with two jobs to simply fund a hobby.

### Moola Now

- The work is immediate and easy.
- It's something already in your repertoire.
- Typically, for a service, it's one-to-one work.
- If it's a product, selling more of what you offer, *now*, may mean running a sale on an existing product or a clearance sale on old inventory.

### Moola Later

- It's more closely aligned with your big vision.
- You may need time to build toward it.
- It may require money up front to develop, but you can recoup costs when you launch.
- You may be working on offers with higher price points that you will need to build up to.
- You may need to develop more credibility and a bigger tribe.

What is your most reliable moola-now method? Do you have a moola-later side project that you want to work on? If so, how much time and money will you need to invest up front in the moola-later project? How can your moola-now method support that?

## MAKE IT EASY FOR PEOPLE TO PAY YOU

If you're not making it easy for people to pay you, then you're losing out on bringing moola in. Even if setting up a new billing service means you pay a small transaction fee or percentage each time a customer uses it, that's still better than no money from no sale.

Here are a few suggestions for making it easy for people to pay you:

- Square (www.squareup.com): You get a small credit-card reader that you plug into the headphone jack of your smartphone or tablet. Take it to events and shows; it's an easy way to accept cards without a merchant account.
- PayPal (www.paypal.com): It's easy to set up, and there's no monthly fee. PayPal takes a cut of each transaction. If you already have a personal account, get a separate business account that's linked to your business checking account.
- E-junkie (www.e-junkie.com): When I first launched my e-book, I used E-junkie to sell it online. It's simple to set up and super-affordable, and it links up with your PayPal account.
- At your bank, get a merchant account and a payment gateway to accept credit cards. There is usually a monthly fee, and the bank takes a percentage of the transaction.
- Include a "buy now" button next to each of your offers on your website. Set up your shopping cart to suggest additional products for your customers to purchase based on what's already in their cart. For example, display product links to what "customers also bought" or "related items." If your system doesn't do that, just follow up with an additional offer in the order confirmation email.
- Set up automatic payments to avoid chasing down clients for monthly moola payments they owe you.

# RIGHT-BRAIN ENTREPRENEUR SPOTLIGHT

Beth DeZiel of Lasso reveals the inspired actions and offers that led up to her best quarter yet.

At the start of 2012, I made a commitment to get my money house in order. I invested in three months' worth of money classes and created a solid foundation. From there, I sprang into action, purchasing QuickBooks, hiring a bookkeeper, opening a Simplified Employee Pension Plan IRA, tracking my money on a weekly basis, teaming up with an accountability buddy, and hiring a CPA.

That was also the year I took a big leap and allowed myself to dream big! I declared that making six figures was one of my top three goals for the year. Although the final number was far from it, the gift of allowing myself the luxury to dream big and take action from an inspired place has paid off in spades.

In January 2013, I did better than doubling, even better than tripling, my income: I (drum roll) quadrupled my income compared to the same time period a year earlier! I also attracted my first corporate client and sold my first top-tier, high-end package. All within the first five months of the year. While I've celebrated the abundance, the real learning has come from accepting the ebb and flow of running a business.

Professional organizer Beth DeZiel knows that wealth is not just about money. She places cherished and meaningful items such as a handmade Valentine from her mom and one of her fancy new business cards in what she calls her money-magnet jar to remind her of the abundance she already attracts into her life.

# RIGHT-BRAIN REFLECTION

We've been talking a lot about how to make more moola, but let's take a moment to reflect from a right-brained perspective. Journal on the following inquiries: How will earning more moola feel? (Really allow yourself to experience the sensations, emotions, and energy of more abundance.) What would become possible for you and your business if you had more moola? (Remember it's usually less about the actual dollar amount and more about what the money gets you and what you can do with it!)

Here are some examples of what fellow right-brain entrepreneurs have shared:

"Making more moola will make me feel free, powerful, energized, and able to make more heartfelt choices, rather than choices based primarily on money."      — Shari Sherman

"I would feel more relaxed and my stress level would go down considerably, because I'd be basking in the glow of having regular massages and spa treatments, a cleaning person, month-long vacations to exotic places, maybe a personal chef so I could lose these nagging ten pounds, a kitchen remodel, a soundproof room so I could play the piano whenever I felt like it, and a dedicated office space so I'm not working out of my living room anymore and can bring someone in to help with some of the administrative stuff. Basically, more moola would mean more time and more comfort in my life."      — Mary Maru Wright

"It would mean that my husband and I could actually have a home of our own, a sanctuary to return to from our travels. We could support local designers to create a space for creativity and peace in our home. I could support my husband's love of music and playing guitar. I would have fewer things, but they would bring more value to my life. It would feel grounded and affirmed. I could invest more in ethical products. I could support more Kickstarter products. I could see my private yoga teacher every six weeks. I would feel both supported and empowered to be making my mark on the world."      — Lou Shackleton

"I want to be able to support my family with a warm home, provide excellent education for girls, set up a program for single moms to send their kids to Waldorf schools, give money to my nonprofit so that home birth can be available to any woman who wants it, travel, see the world, meet people, and honor natural beauty."      — Helene Rose

"I will be able to contribute to my family monetarily, pay down some of our debt, and take everyone to Hawaii."      — Monica Garcia

"The added income would not only validate what I do, but it would also give me the confidence to keep going. It would take some stress off and allow for better creative energy."

      — Desiree Habicht

## What Will More Moola Get You?

Besides your day-to-day expenses, there are, I imagine, things you probably want or need in your personal life. Part of having sustainable success is letting your money work for you. When you're working way too hard for your money — or worse, working too hard for no money — eventually you'll run yourself and your business into the ground. There was a time when I was resentfully writing checks to my vendors for more than I was paying myself, and meanwhile my roof was leaking and thriving weeds made up my sorry "front lawn." I couldn't go on this way, so I reconfigured my team, removed other expenses, and eventually was able to start investing more in myself again. I got the roof fixed and, since rest and relaxation are important to me, even treated myself to a new king-size bed.

What things do you want in your personal life? This is your wish list. It's helpful to have a sense of how much moola you'd need for each item so that it will help inform your overall moola goal and determine how much you pay yourself. Here are a couple of examples with moola estimates just for the sake of illustration: Go on a ten-day Maui vacation with your sweetie in spring ($3,000). Replace old car in twelve months ($5,000 down payment and $350/month for five years).

What business needs do you want to invest in? Your business must be tended if it is to grow. How much will the new purchases cost? And when? Here are some examples, including estimated numbers for illustration purposes (do some detective work and find prices for what you're looking for):

- Hire an assistant next quarter (start off with ten hours per month at $35/hour, totaling $350/month).
- Get professional headshots next month ($300).
- Get a new laptop by the end of the year ($1,500).
- Purchase high-end equipment that will streamline your production flow or allow you to produce even better-quality work in the next two years ($1,200).

- Revamp your website next year ($3,000).
- Create a prototype for a new product ($1,000).
- Implement more robust tools and infrastructure in two years ($3,000).
- Open up a new work space in three years ($1,200/month for rent and utilities).
- Print new business cards or brochures for an event this month ($300).
- Rent a booth at a popular trade show at the end of the year ($750).
- Travel to an important conference for your industry next spring ($2,000 for your airfare, hotel, and event ticket).

Which items do you really want to invest in this year for your personal life? Which items do you really want to invest in this year for your business?

Artist Virginia Simpson-Magruder of Kentucky Girl Designs wanted a studio where she could meet the public and they could see her work. She said, "Getting the space motivated me to set financial goals for myself so that I could cover rent, materials, and so on. It also assisted me in confronting my fears and self-limiting beliefs about what I was capable of achieving, and this permitted me to choose to stretch and grow."

How much do these items add up to? Keep this number in mind when you look at your moola goal for the year. Do you need to increase your target number to fund these things? Remember, part of sustainable success is being able to invest in yourself, give back, and enjoy the fruits of your labor, so take these desired investments into account.

What you'll need:

- Plain or colored paper
- Scissors
- Markers or colorful pens
- Washi tape (optional)
- Magazines or catalog clippings, or color printouts from images online (optional)
- Glue stick (optional)
- Glitter glue (optional)

Choose a few of the items on your personal or business wish list that you want to invest in this year. For each item, create a "gift certificate" made out to you and write in the estimated value. You can include a picture to represent what you want to invest in or simply add a description.

Post your gift certificates where you can see them so they'll remind you what you can use your earnings for. Then, once you've brought in the moola needed, "redeem" your gift certificate and enjoy your reward. Keep the redeemed gift certificates in a special envelope or box to remind you of the abundance you've brought into your life.

Rather go digital? Pin your wish list items on Pinterest or create a vision board on your iPhone app (my favorite is by my pal Carla White, the Happy Tapper Vision Board app).

Having tangible goals like the ones shown on these Wish-List Gift Certificates can make the numbers that you track feel more real.

## Make Your Moola Work for You

Owners of sustainable businesses make their money work for them. Make sure you're looking at the numbers and making educated decisions to keep yourself and your company thriving.

- Review your Entrepreneurial Ecosystem (in particular the stem and leaves).
- Identify where you are on the Multiple Moola-Making Methods Map.
- Reflect on how having more moola will make you feel.
- Make your wish list gift certificates.

 **LEFT-BRAIN CHECKLIST**

Your left brain appreciates keeping track of the steps you've taken toward your sustained success.

- ❏ I have picked a moola-making path to focus on.
- ❏ I have enough leaves on my Business Flower to equal the moola goal on my stem.
- ❏ I've made it easy for people to pay me.
- ❏ I am working on my moola-now activities to generate cash flow.
- ❏ I am allocating time for my moola-later activities to maximize my future earning potential.

# PART IV

# SUSTAINING YOUR SUCCESS

# In Good Company

## Growing Your Team and Getting Support

As a right-brain entrepreneur you probably wear many hats — from those of creator and copywriter all the way to those of bookkeeper and scheduler. I bet you love doing your craft, and that you probably loathe the left-brain business tasks. Believe me, I'd rather be drawing colorful doodles than drawing up dry legal contracts. But just because I dislike those left-brain details doesn't mean I can ignore them, even if I desperately want to.

Ask yourself what you're truly passionate about. Why did you start your creative business in the first place? Chances are, you're passionate about everything but the tedious tasks that are driving you crazy! You started your business to bring beauty and creativity into the world, not to be buried in bank statements or endless administrative to-dos. You want to focus on doing what you love, where your greatest gifts are, and on what's most profitable.

If you've been in business for a while and you want to grow to the next level, there will most likely come a time when you need to switch from flying solo to building a team. It won't be physically possible for you to do everything yourself anymore. You may not be ready to hire help right away, either because you're still learning the ropes, or you want to stay lean for as long as you can, or you're focused on maintaining a positive cash flow — and that's smart. Still, keeping in mind where you're headed, and what type of support you'll need in order to get there, will let you be on the lookout for good people to work with when the time is right.

This chapter covers ideas on outsourcing, suggestions for hiring and getting support, and thoughts about how to expand your team through strategic alliances. You'll also hear from fellow right-brain entrepreneurs about how they've learned to ask for help, delegate, and collaborate in order to make their big visions come true.

## Review Your Entrepreneurial Ecosystem

Take a look at your Business Flower from the Entrepreneurial Ecosystem exercise. There are several places in the Ecosystem where we assessed the support you're receiving. In particular, look at the sun, where you noted expert guidance and support. Do you have the right people to turn to for those?

Look at the watering can, which represents emotional support. Are there encouraging people in your circle who will offer you a shoulder to cry on or act as cheerleaders to celebrate with?

Look at the soil. Do you have the knowledge and resources needed to take your business to the next level? If not, is there someone you can partner with to get that?

## How I Started to Grow My Team

When I first started out, I handled most of the business details myself because that made sense for my fledgling business. My hubby helped, and thankfully still does, with all things tech- and research-related. After a few years, though, I realized that in order to grow my business to the next level (and to stay sane), I needed to invest in some help.

The first person I hired was an accountant who set up QuickBooks. He trained me in the basics so I could take care of invoices and monthly reconciliations. It was great because having hands-on experience with the ins and outs of my moola helped me understand what was going on in my business. But then when I could no longer deal with the complexity of the books (in other words when I made a big mess of QuickBooks), I hired a bookkeeper to clean up the files and handle all future bookkeeping.

Occasionally I worked with a graphic designer on projects, and I enlisted the service of a branding consultant and copywriter. And after about four years of working solo, I hired my first virtual assistant. Over time, I've learned to outsource when it makes sense. My creative cohorts help me focus on the things I enjoy, and they get to focus on what they enjoy.

Lou Shackleton formed her not-for-profit organization, the You Can Hub, with former work colleagues. Even though they already knew each other, the team used the StrengthsFinder 2.0 tool to understand each other's unique gifts. They collaboratively crafted the organization's values and vision, and they work together to ensure that all aspects of the You Can Hub align with those.

If you're used to doing everything on your own, it can be challenging to know what to start outsourcing. You may think it's easier to just do it yourself. And yes, sometimes it is easier, especially in the beginning while your business is still finding its way. But as you grow and the complexity of your business increases, you may discover that your day-to-day work has shifted and you can't serve more clients or make more of your goods unless you take some tasks off your plate.

Here are some things to consider if you want to identify potential tasks to outsource:

### What Are You Not That Good At? Or What Requires Expertise?

What tasks do you lack the skills or aptitude for, no matter how hard you try? Maybe when it comes to anything computer related? (Yes, I'm talking about myself here, since my husband is always having to fix my laptop for me, my websites, my email, you name it!) For challenges like this, it makes sense to let those who know what they're doing help you.

What aspects of your business need someone with specific expertise or experience? For example, I always look to my attorney for legal advice and my accountant for tax-related answers. No matter how accustomed I get to reading and signing contracts, I'm still going to have a lawyer look over the fine print to ensure that my intellectual property and business are protected. And one year when I was the "lucky" recipient of a random audit, you can bet that the first person I called was my accountant; thankfully, he guided me through the whole process.

Your business may also require expertise because it's naturally growing in a new direction where you have less direct experience. Perhaps you're expanding to a new geographic territory, you've attracted a new customer base, or you need to develop partnerships in a new industry. Recently, I've been getting more requests from nonprofit organizations interested in licensing my work. Since I don't have any experience in the nonprofit world, and I don't have the bandwidth to familiarize myself deeply with a new industry, I knew I needed to find someone with a not-for-profit background who could speak their language and help me explore the opportunities. Where in your business could you leverage someone with specific knowledge and experience?

## What Drives You Crazy, Pisses You Off, or Makes You Cross-Eyed?

Are there certain tasks in your work that you simply can't stand? If there's that much negativity associated with it, it really is not a good use of your time and energy. You'll get so resentful every time you have to deal with it that in time it will drain you and prevent you from doing good work. I must confess that one thing that used to drive me crazy was answering emails about tech issues, like when people were unable to log in to a course or had trouble downloading a file. I would dread opening my email. If I got several of them around the same time, you can bet I complained about it to my husband every chance I could. Not a good use of my time or his! One of the first things I did when I got a virtual assistant was to have her respond to technical questions. Once I moved those off my plate, my inbox felt lighter. Take responsibility for your reactions — bad ones usually signal a task you shouldn't be doing. What do you find yourself complaining about often?

## What Takes You Too Long, When Your Time Could Be Better Spent Elsewhere?

While I like to doodle for fun, I knew I would be better served by hiring my übertalented friend Kate to illustrate my first book and this one. I know enough about scanning images and using design programs that I can get by when making quick graphics and icons. But had I attempted to do all the drawings in this book, they wouldn't have looked nearly as good as hers, I would have been superstressed trying to get everything just so, and I would have wasted my time muddling through Photoshop and Illustrator. By hiring a professional, I got high-quality work. I also got to focus on other things that required my personal touch, such as writing the manuscript and managing the marketing. And I got to collaborate with one of my favorite people while supporting her in her business.

## What Comes Easy but Doesn't Inspire Your Passion, or Keeps You from More Profitable Work?

Maybe you used to love assembling your beaded necklaces, and you're still really good at it, but you've become bored by the routine task. Designing new products excites you more, and you know it will lead to more opportunities for income, especially since you're dreaming up a higher-end jewelry line. But since you have orders to fill, you spend your time on that rather than on developing new, probably more profitable offerings. This could be an opportunity to get an apprentice. Teach her skills, and she can do those tasks while you focus on your new moola-making methods.

## A Peek into What I Own and What I Outsource

As an example, let me show you what I currently do for myself and what I outsource. Of course, this is just a snapshot, and by the time you read this I will probably have delegated even more.

### What I Do Myself

- Strategy and vision: Where do I want my company to be in a year, five years, ten years? What impact do I want to make?
- Business planning and development: I identify and make the most of potential opportunities.
- Strategic partnership development and management: Who are the key collaborators and companies that I want to partner with? How can I cultivate those relationships and negotiate contracts and agreements with the help of advisors and lawyers?

- I write my books and newsletters and design and develop course materials, workshops, programs, and products.
- I coach and mentor individuals.
- I coach and lead groups, online communities, and workshops. (I get some help with this from fellow facilitators and circle coaches.)
- I do speaking engagements.
- I manage the moola.
  - Billing clients, collecting payment, and paying vendors (with some help from my assistant)
  - Getting my statements and receipts to my bookkeeper monthly and answering her questions
  - Financial projections/budget and reviewing financial reports (monthly profit and loss, product sales, cash forecast, and so on)
- I get the word out.
  - Social media (with some help from my assistant)
  - Participating in guest interviews and writing guest posts
- I manage sales.
  - Crafting and making offers
  - Creating love-letter sales pages and subsequent communications
  - Designing and updating my websites (with some help from others)
- Scheduling: Since I like being in control of my own time and schedule, I manage my own calendar; but I automate as much as possible using an online scheduling system.

## What I Currently Outsource

- Reconciling my accounts in QuickBooks
- Filing business taxes and sales and use taxes
- Legal assistance for registering trademarks and creating, reviewing, and negotiating contracts

- Graphic design and illustration for print and creative projects
- Technical and video broadcasting support
- Workshop facilitation (through my licensed Right-Brain Business Plan facilitators)
- Some group coaching and e-course facilitation
- Some sales and business development
- Photography: headshots, action shots, product shots (except for the product and promotional photos I take myself because it's fun)
- Administrative tasks
    - Answering general customer-service or information-seeking emails
    - Setting up online groups and courses
    - Managing access to online communities
    - Managing and scheduling social media
    - Coordinating and scheduling our contributor blog posts
    - Creating and scheduling emails and reminders for various lists
    - Uploading audio and video recordings, chat logs, and other materials
    - Setting up products for e-commerce
    - Managing affiliates
    - Coordinating joint venture and guest speaker opportunities
    - Getting copies and binders made
    - Ordering supplies
    - Event coordination and catering of food for events
- Assembling tangible products
- Shipping products
- Documenting Smooth Sailing Systems
- Transcription
- Cleaning my house
- Some meals and other food preparation (organic, locally made food that I get delivered because I can't stand cooking)

## What I've Outsourced in the Past

- Copyediting
- Copywriting
- Proofreading
- Brand consulting
- Website design
- Logo development

## Knowing When to Outsource

Yes, it can be hard to fathom paying someone else to help you in your business when you may not be earning a lot yet. Learning to delegate is an important business leadership skill, though, and the more you practice this earlier on, the easier it will be when you really need to grow your team. And when you reach a certain level in your business, investing in help can actually let you earn more in the long-term.

Start with a small, contained project just to see what it's like to delegate or to try out a possible cohort who might help you. You can also experiment with bartering or with hiring an intern. And there are some websites like Fiverr.com or TaskRabbit.com that can connect you with potential candidates.

> **TIP**
> Check with your tax accountant or visit the IRS website to determine if you need to hire an employee rather than an independent contractor, since there are certain tax implications for each.

Outsourcing may be your next step when you find you're spending more time on administrative tasks than on moola-making activities. Don't wait until you're completely overwhelmed or exhausted. Bringing on someone new to help out will take some up-front time and energy, so you'll want to have the capacity to give that and start off on the right foot.

Be careful of outsourcing too much too soon, though. Constantly paying your vendors more than you're paying yourself, or more than you're able to invest back into the business, doesn't promote your business's long-term health. So start small and know how much you need to bring in to cover the expense.

At first, coach Tiffany Han was shocked to find that the business plan she developed using the Right-Brain Business Plan was nothing but "words, words, words." What it helped her realize, though, is that she really is a writer. That aha moment both prompted her to refocus her business and helped her decide to hire her first creative cohort — a graphic designer who makes beautiful images to accompany her words.

### EXERCISE
## Who Does What: Determining What to Outsource

In part 1 of the Who Does What chart, put a check in the "Me" column for the functions you want responsibility for. These should be the things you love and that are the heart of your business. Refer to your helping-hands wish list and put a check in the "Others" column for things you want help with. If these are things you don't want help with right away, add the date you expect to ask for it, or say "six months from now" or "a year from now," for example. If you know the name of your potential helper, you can include it here. If a role doesn't apply to your business, put "N/A." And feel free to add your own categories.

| FUNCTION OR ROLE | ME<br>I want full responsibility for this,<br>I'm good at it, or I enjoy doing it | OTHERS<br>I can't stand this, need expert help,<br>or simply want to delegate this |
|---|---|---|
| Strategy and vision | | |
| Planning to grow my business and make the most of potential opportunities | | |
| Research and development for new products and services | | |
| Production (such as making the jewelry, art, kits, and so on) | | |
| Content development (which, for a service provider, could include writing, developing, and packaging your services) | | |
| Providing the services to customers (for a service-based business) | | |
| Marketing to reach more people | | |
| Sales to increase money coming in | | |
| Operations to keep my business running smoothly | | |
| Administrative tasks such as paperwork, scheduling, and other tactical work | | |
| Finances, including the financial big picture, projections, and planning | | |
| Billing and collecting payment | | |
| Bookkeeping, including recording financial transactions and reconciling accounts | | |
| Managing people: providing guidance, direction, and feedback to my contractors or employees | | |
| Staffing my company, including hiring and firing workers | | |
| Training and educating my team on how work gets done in my business | | |

Use part 2 of the Who Does What chart to help you determine whether you need to hire specific outside services and by when. Some of these may be necessary a year or more ahead of time, but it's good to plan ahead and be on the lookout for good candidates so you're not scrambling when you're ready to hire.

| OUTSIDE SERVICES | DO I NEED? (Yes/No) | WHEN? | WHO? |
|---|---|---|---|
| Attorney | | | |
| Accountant | | | |
| Bookkeeper | | | |
| Administrative assistant or virtual assistant | | | |
| Branding consultant | | | |
| Marketing consultant | | | |
| Publicist or PR manager | | | |
| Graphic designer | | | |
| Copywriter | | | |
| Proofreader or editor | | | |
| Web developer | | | |
| Tech guru | | | |
| Business consultant or coach | | | |
| Photographer | | | |
| Sales rep | | | |
| Agent | | | |
| Intern | | | |

## RIGHT-BRAIN ENTREPRENEUR SPOTLIGHT

Fiction-writing coach Beth Barany built her team by first hiring a virtual assistant and someone to handle QuickBooks. But the significant shift came when Beth clearly claimed her passion for creating content and began delegating most everything else. Beth says, "Delegating has presented a big learning curve because I'm a bit of a control freak, and because it has felt as if the time it takes to explain something is the same amount of time it would have taken me to *do* the task. But I've learned that once I've trained someone, it takes only a short time to request that the task be done. Then I can go back to focusing on my core work."

Whether you decide to bring an official employee into your company, or you're partnering with your first freelancer, here are some suggestions for how to go about finding the right person to support you.

### Be Clear about Where You Need Help

List the tasks you want to delegate. Even if you don't have an ongoing need, perhaps you have an upcoming project that could benefit from expert advice or an extra pair of hands. Maybe you're launching a new website, developing a new workshop, or preparing for a big art show.

### Be Clear about the Perfect Person to Help You with These Tasks

What qualities and experience does she possess? What are her values, and how do they align with yours? Do you need a local person so you can meet face-to-face, or can she be anywhere in the world? Is this someone who will help with a specific project, or do you want to groom an employee who can grow with you? Get out your journal and write about this perfect person as if you've already been working with her. Describe what you enjoy most about your partnership.

### Write a Job Description or a Classified Ad

Even if you don't plan on sharing it or running an advertisement, this activity will help you articulate what you're looking for. See page 170 for a short exercise and example.

### Be on the Lookout for Good Recommendations

To find candidates, ask friends and colleagues for referrals, network, and search online at places such as Assistu.com (for a virtual assistant) or Elance.com (for a virtual assistant, designer, or other freelancer). Even if you're not yet ready to hire someone, get to know possible candidates casually. That way you're not choosing someone out of desperation when you need to hire at the last minute. (I've been there; it didn't turn out well.)

## Interview at Least Two People

That way you can get a feel for who would be the best fit. Yes, this takes time to do, and it is time well spent. Ask a set of questions to help you gather the information you need. Inquire about each candidate's process, turnaround time, rates, and anything else you need to know in order to make your decision. You may even ask to speak to past or current clients. Do your homework, but also make sure you follow your gut. You want to have a good feeling about working with this person. When you decide to hire someone, spend some time during your first meeting so you can get to know each other and learn about the other's working style and expectations.

> **RIGHT-BRAIN BOOSTER**
>
> Surround yourself with a great team. The more great people you surround yourself with, the more they'll help connect you with other great people. (Such people seem to hang around each other!) And do your part to connect great people with each other. It's good karma.

## Keep the Lines of Communication Open

Once you start working with someone, both of you can give feedback and raise any concerns before they snowball. Depending on how your work relationship is structured, you may want to connect weekly via email or phone to discuss your progress or answer questions. And pay attention to indicators that things may be off — for example, you start to find too many errors in his work, or he's making mistakes that are costing you money, or his deliverables are late. If things can't be resolved after conversations, don't be afraid to move on. It may feel like an awkward or uncomfortable "breakup," but be willing to start looking again if it's not working out. Don't settle for less. You'll be happier when you find the right person!

## Continue to Develop Your Working Relationships with Your Outside Partners

Show your appreciation for their good work. Write them nice thank-you cards. Let them know how much they are helping you and what you love about working with them. The more specific you can be, the better. So, for example, don't say simply "You're great!" but rather: "Thank you for helping me complete the project on time and on budget. I really appreciate how you anticipated my need for a backup plan, and that you came up with a creative solution when we hit those unexpected challenges." Help your outside partners expand their businesses by referring your friends and colleagues to them.

## ACTION ACCELERATOR
Delegate at least one thing this week. This will help you build your asking-for-help muscle.

## RIGHT-BRAIN ENTREPRENEUR SPOTLIGHT

Bindi Shah, the owner of Amayana, a health and well-being business, found that sometimes help is right under your nose. Bindi is a meditation teacher and life coach based in Britain who runs meditation circles and workshops out of her home. During one of her classes, she mentioned that she was looking for a housecleaner. A few months later, a student checked in to see if she had found someone yet. Bindi hadn't yet, and the student offered to help because she wanted her beloved teacher to focus on teaching rather than tidying up.

To keep their student-teacher relationship "clean," so to speak, they do not barter — Bindi pays the student for her housecleaning services, and the student continues to pay for the classes she attends. Bindi says, "It is all working out really well. Even though she's not a professional cleaner, she cleans even better than the cleaners I had before. I now have more energy and time, including a full Monday to work on my business!"

Look at both completed parts of your Who Does What chart and pick one of the activities you've decided to outsource. To help you elaborate more on what you're looking for, write up a classified ad seeking a creative cohort. List all the qualities, experience, background, and skills you want this person to have. Whether you actually publish an ad or not, writing these things down on paper will help you get clear about the type of person and support you want.

After I wrote this classified ad seeking someone who could sell my licensing program to nonprofit organizations, I soon realized that a person in my circle was a possible collaborator and partner for this next stage of my business growth.

April 4, 2013

helping hands wish list

A Sales person who could generate leaDs with organizations to license RBBP work, follow up with inouiries /requests that come in, and negotiate contracts & close the Sales. Someone experienceD in Licensing, contracts, selling to organizations and non-profits. Someone who really gets the RBBP approach, brand & message & who would finD prospects aligneD well w/ that. A gooD listener & collaborator who i could trust to represent me & my company. they could also work well w/ my legal advisors to help navigate some of those conversations. work on some kind of commission structure. Help me expanD my reach in Big ways!

Meditation teacher and life coach Bindi Shah articulated the areas she wanted to focus on in her business and envisioned how she'd get help for the rest.

## Attract Potential Partners

Another way to grow your team is to find collaborative partners. Strategic alliances are a great way to expand your reach and get more done than you could do on your own. Whether you want to team up with a larger organization, buddy with another solopreneur who has complementary offerings, or gather several guests or collaborators together for a project, there are some points to consider.

## RIGHT-BRAIN ENTREPRENEUR SPOTLIGHT

Life and business coach Tiffany Han spearheaded a project called "Love Letters" that she collaborated on with twelve artists. Together they created a product that is delivered each month, one that includes an inspiring art print, an inspiring love letter, and a coaching exercise from Tiffany. She gives us a peek into how she corralled her cohorts for this joint effort:

Once I'd sketched out the idea, I reached out to my good friend Jess Swift, a professional artist. Since I had no idea how licensing works, she was a fantastic resource. I would have been flailing on my own! After Jess assured me that, yes, it was a great idea and, yes, she did want to participate, she taught me how licensing typically works and helped me come up with my pricing and payment schedule.

I made up my dream list of artists, some of whom I was lucky enough to already know. Others were strangers, and I started reaching out to them. Some said yes right away; some said no right away, and some I never heard back from. Tenacity is key! Once I had some folks signed on, I did not hesitate to drop their names so that people would know this project was legit. It can't hurt to know people who know people!

One thing I would have done differently would have been to use a much shorter email to introduce the project and ask artists to participate. I was trying to explain all the details of the project so they would fall in love with it, but I think short and sweet is better. Also, when reaching out to strangers, flattery is essential! Give them a reason to like you right away!

## Know What You Have to Offer

Perhaps you have original content, a new idea, a sought-after product, or certain skills, resources, or connections. Be clear about the value you're bringing to the table. You may be thinking to yourself, "I don't have anything that someone else would consider valuable" or "Other people have more reach, talent, and so on than I have; why would anyone want to partner with me?" Instead, think about what you do have to offer that is unique and which could be what your perfect partner really needs. Know your strengths. Also know your core message, so that you can make sure it aligns with what your partner stands for.

## RIGHT-BRAIN BOOSTER

Allow yourself to dream big when it comes to support. In the *Right-Brain Business Plan* book (pages 124–25), I introduced an exercise for creating a helping-hands wish list. Write down all the things you would love to get help with in your business (and your life, for that matter).

### Articulate What You Want from a Strategic Partner

What would you like your cohort to contribute to the partnership? What would complement your offering? What qualities do you want in your cohort? It's important to find a good fit; otherwise you'll run into problems working together.

### Build Your Relationship First

Cultivate your connection before entering into partnerships. Effective collaboration requires a foundation of trust and communication, and this develops over time. I'm more likely to collaborate with someone I already know and trust. Just as you're not likely to ask someone to marry you on a first date, it's good to get to know people first and then build up to your request to collaborate. Get

## LEFT-BRAIN CHILL PILL

Lean into support. If you're used to going it alone, it can be a challenge to simply receive. But that's partly why you're looking for help, right? Be open to assistance so you can stop bearing the burden all by your lonesome.

to know prospective collaborators on social media and interact with them. Maybe send emails letting them know how much their work has helped you. Then, when the time is right, reach out with your invitation.

## Ask Gracefully

Once you've found a potential collaborator, tell her why you are reaching out to her, why you'd love working with her, and why you think she's the perfect person for the project. Be clear and direct with your request. Explain how you think this opportunity can benefit her, so she understands what's in it for her. People are busy, so keep your request short and sweet. If you have a mutual contact, ask that person to facilitate an introduction. Make sure you give your mutual contact some context for your request so she can vouch for you with specific words of support for your project. If the potential partner you've reached out to turns down your offer, please follow up anyway and thank her for taking the time to reply. This is still part of being in a relationship. If you don't close the loop and acknowledge the reply, it can make your initial effusive invitation seem inauthentic. You don't want to burn bridges or leave a bad impression with someone who could be a future collaborator when the time is right.

> **TIP**
>
> Make it easy for your prospective collaborators to do their homework. If you have a product, book, blog, or some other way for people to safely get to know you and your work from afar, it will give them a taste of you before they connect with you.

## Create a Clear Agreement

Not every situation requires hiring a lawyer to draft a fancy formal contract. Simply get on paper in layperson's language what each party's expectations, roles, responsibilities, and rights are. And if your partnership does require a formal contract (because there's a lot at stake in terms of money and intellectual property for both parties), it's still helpful to first write in layperson's terms what both parties want and then hand that over to an attorney to put into legalese. Some considerations for an agreement include: Who owns what? What can you sell? What can the other party sell? Is there profit sharing? How are expenses handled? Is one person handling more of the administrative costs because she has the infrastructure, and will that person then get more of the profit? How will disputes be handled? When does the relationship end? Make sure you both accept the agreement, and then sign it to seal the deal.

# RIGHT-BRAIN ENTREPRENEUR SPOTLIGHT

Brighid O'Shaughnessy is the founder and executive artistic director of Erasing the Distance, a Chicago-based nonprofit dedicated to shedding light on mental health issues through theater. I've seen her go from being simply one fiery woman with a dream to leading a thriving organization that has touched more than forty thousand people. Brighid says of her organization's growth:

When I started Erasing the Distance in 2005, I played every role. I collected every story. I transcribed and shaped every interview into a performance-ready monologue. I then directed, produced, and acted in every show we ever did. And that was just on the programming side. I also wrote every grant, drafted every budget, built a board from the ground up, and cut every paycheck. In 2009, though, I began to have the funds to build a more consistent "staffing" team; and boy, was that a shift.

For example, I'm not savvy in all things graphic and digital. With the help of a team, we got a beautiful new website and high-quality materials for prospective clients. Our branding became more polished and consistent. Others boosted our Facebook, blog, and e-blast presence, which expanded our network of supporters beyond simply those who could be reached by word of mouth. We launched ourselves to a whole other level of professionalism and legitimacy.

My role has changed immensely. While I occasionally still implement programming directly, I am now in more of a management and training role. I have a managing director, communications director, and production manager to handle other duties I used to juggle. Our staff now consists of two full-time paid positions, two part-time paid positions, a team of more than thirty artists, a mental health advisory board, and dozens of volunteers, as well as our traditional board of directors.

The skills it takes to build a nonprofit from the ground up are not necessarily the same as the ones it takes to be an effective manager of an organization and people on a day-to-day basis. I find myself having to fill my toolbox with new skills, and this continues to stretch me in all sorts of interesting and sometimes difficult ways.

That said, our impact and reach is far greater now than anything I could have achieved alone. We could not have reached the number of people we have, as professionally and sensitively as we have, without the collective effort of our team. We are much closer than ever before to becoming an organization that could truly live on beyond the founder. This is a great step in the direction of true sustainability, and it's incredibly exciting.

## Let Go of Control (or at Least Loosen Your Grip)

Allow each contributor to own her piece and lend her unique talents. You'll end up with something far richer that way.

## Keep the Lines of Communication Open

### TIP

When you do your quarterly reviews, make sure you check in with your team. Do you have the right people in place? Are there relationships you need to work on? Is there an area where you will need more support soon?

Have checkpoints. You can use the simple Stop, Start, Continue structure to help frame your check-ins. (Download the Stop, Start, Continue illustrated play sheet at www.rightbrainbusiness plan.com/rbbiz.) Identify what's working and what's not, and make adjustments. And after the collaborative project is done, debrief each other on how it went. Remember, this is another opportunity for learning.

## Go Team!

Whether you decide to try delegating work to an intern or to expand your one-person show to a team of twenty, or you simply try out a strategic alliance during your next launch, it's important to be clear about where you could use help the most. The more you can clarify (and get) the type of support you need, the more you'll pave the way for your sustained success.

## Recap of Activities

- Review your Entrepreneurial Ecosystem (in particular the sun, watering can, and soil).
- Fill out the Who Does What chart.
- Create a classified ad for a creative cohort.

## LEFT-BRAIN CHECKLIST

Your left brain appreciates keeping track of the steps you've taken toward your sustained success.

- ☐ I have identified the activities I want to own (including what I love doing and what's most profitable).
- ☐ I know what I want to outsource or delegate and when.
- ☐ I have written a classified ad for a creative cohort and have started a search.
- ☐ I know what I have to offer in a strategic partnership.
- ☐ I am reaching out and developing relationships with key cohorts.

# Smooth Sailing Systems

## Make Day-to-Day Operations a Breeze

One of the keys to growing your business with more ease is having a solid foundation of effective and efficient day-to-day operations. While that may not sound as sexy or exciting as dreaming up your next inspiring product, having your left-brain details in order can actually free up your energy to be more creative. Starting from scratch each time you do a task is taxing. Instead, streamline your efforts, eliminate rework, and reap the rewards.

Your Smooth Sailing Systems include the infrastructure, processes, and tools that help you run your business smoothly. When these are in place, everyday activities such as managing orders, collecting payments, delivering products, interacting with your tribe, marketing your offers, and supporting your customers all become a breeze. Of course, not everything will run perfectly all the time, but

*smooth sailing systems*

your Smooth Sailing Systems will give you the capacity to continuously improve your business.

## An Investment in Your Future

It may take a bit of extra effort in the beginning to set things up; but rest assured, there is a payoff. The work you've done up to this point to reach out to your right peeps, produce your products, craft your offers, write your sales-page love letters, and implement your launch plan is actually an investment in your future, when you can turn those steps into replicable templates, systems, and processes. Pretty soon you'll develop your own proven recipes for success that will help you bring in more moola with less effort. Repeatable processes and reusable moola-making methods generate more stability, predictability, and reliability in your business. And this, in turn, lays the groundwork for more innovation and growth. Sounds like sustainable success to me!

> **TIP**
>
> When you're still new to a line of work, you may be in the process of figuring out what systems you need — and that's okay. Stay lean for as long as you can. That way, you can understand the ins and outs of your business before you prematurely invest in more expensive infrastructure that may not meet your requirements.

Your Smooth Sailing Systems are unique to your business. This chapter offers some suggestions about what to document or systematize and some prompts to get you started. However, how you do it and to what level of detail depend on your situation, so use your own creative license.

## Repurpose, and Reap the Rewards

If someone invited you to make an offer to thousands or even tens of thousands of new people, would you be ready to take advantage of the opportunity? Do you have the necessary systems and processes in place to make that happen easily and on short notice?

Fortunately, I had just such an opportunity, and because I have my Smooth Sailing Systems in place, I was able to bring in an unexpected five figures after doing a low-key, two-week-long launch. I was invited to lead a live, three-day workshop that would be broadcast over the web, and I knew that during the event I'd have permission to make a follow-on offer. Since I was busy prepping for the main workshop, I didn't have time to craft a brand-new offer. Taking a Mr.-Sketch, keep-it-simple, approach, I chose to run a limited-time special on one of my related programs. My assistant helped me reuse parts of previous love letters and sign-up forms, and she set up a coupon code in my e-commerce system. I wrote a bit of marketing copy and a handful of emails, and I led a one-hour free video chat, where I made the offer. By using what had worked in the past, I was able to bring in an extra chunk of change that wasn't originally on my moola map for the month. Pretty cool, right?

## Documenting Your Repeatable Recipes for Success

Documenting your processes is one of the simplest ways to get your Smooth Sailing Systems going. Now you may think, "I know how to run this project like the back of my hand, so why should I bother writing it down?" Or: "I've been producing this item for ages; what's the point of explaining the steps on paper?" Well, the more sophisticated your business becomes — as you add new offers, products, and customers — the more challenging it will be to keep track of all the details in your head. And if at some point if you want to delegate tasks, it's a lot easier to train people when you have procedures to refer to. In my previous example about the lucrative follow-on offer, my assistant already knew how to handle her tasks because of documented processes.

You don't need to write up every last detail, since that's probably not the best use of your time. Just record some high-level bullet points to help you remember key tasks, decision points, and dependencies. Also note any weird things to watch out for and any work-arounds or short-cuts. You're basically creating a cheat sheet, recipe, or "honey-do" list to refer to when you need it.

### Write Your Honey-Do List

While I was growing up, my mom kept a honey-do list pinned up in the kitchen. When she thought of something she wanted my dad to fix, or a household chore she needed him to take care of, she would write it down. You know, things like: "fix the side gate," "replace the shutters," or "mow the lawn." It was her simple system for tracking and communicating what needed to happen around the house.

**TIP**

If you're not documenting in real time because you've already finished the task or project, sometimes reviewing your notes or email exchanges can help you piece together what worked.

When you record your processes, think of them as a honey-do list for your future self or your team. In a simple Word document or shared file, write down your process as you go. Some things to consider:

- What needs to happen? What is the process? (You can see some types of processes in the next section.)
- How often does it happen? When does it happen?
- What needs to happen daily, weekly, monthly, quarterly, or yearly?
- What steps are involved?
- What do you have to set up? Are there certain technical things that need to be done?
- Is there an order in which things have to be done?
- What materials or resources do you need? How many and when?
- What information is needed, and who can supply it? For

example, what account logins, prices, amounts, dates, and descriptions are required?

- Who needs to be involved?
- What are the decision points? Is there an approval process?
- Are there things to watch out for?

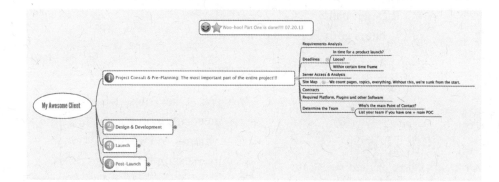

Mind maps are an effective way to visually document your business processes. Writer and web designer Mari Pfeiffer gives us a peek into the process she follows with her clients.

## Types of Processes

Which processes you document depends on your business. For example, if you make goods, you may have certain processes and systems for use during production, while sourcing raw materials, and while shipping. If you're a service provider, you may need to manage client projects, track your billable hours, or schedule sessions or classes.

Following are some types of processes that you may need to document in your business. Included are some prompts to help you recognize what types of details to capture. This is by no means an exhaustive list. Use it to spark your own thinking and planning.

## Payment and Moola

- How will you accept payment?
- How will you handle manual payments or payment plans?
- How will you track your billable hours?
- How will you invoice? What's the time frame?
- How will you handle returns or refunds?
- How can you set up discounts, coupons, or sales?
- Do you have an affiliate program set up? If so, what are the commissions? How often do affiliates get paid? How do they get paid?
- What is your bookkeeping system?

## Launch Plans

### RIGHT-BRAIN BOOSTER

Use creativity, color, and visuals to make your procedures fun and functional. Color-code the steps. Draw mind maps. Add in images. Use process flows or diagrams to visually represent left-brain information, especially if steps need to happen in a certain order or there are key decision points. Include screenshots to show exactly what needs to happen, and supplement them with written instructions or callouts. Shoot a short video of yourself demonstrating how to do a task.

- What key messages do you need to communicate? To whom? And when? See launch plan examples on pages 112–13.
- What media do you use for getting the word out? What works best?
- What product, promotion, or list-building setups do you use?
- Who will be involved in the launch? What do they need to do? What information or resources should be provided to them? What is the timing?
- Are there marketing materials (such as email copy, marketing copy, web pages, graphics, and love letters) that you can repurpose for a future launch? Are those easy to find in your systems?

- What pieces or sections need to be updated when you launch again? And what can be reused as is?

### Customer Relationship Management

- How do you keep track of who your top customers are?
- Which customers do you need to stay in closer contact with?
- What stage of the sales cycle are they in? What follow-up is needed? (This is especially important to be aware of when your offerings require long lead times or applications or approval.)
- How do you track referrals, and how do you reward the customers who refer customers to you?

### Scheduling

- What are your hours of business operation?
- What calendar system do you use?
- How can clients schedule appointments with you?
- Does your company's schedule need to be posted somewhere so others can see things, such as classes or events? Who will update the schedule and how often?

### Vendors and Procurement

- Who do you buy your raw materials and other supplies from?
- How often do you need to replenish supplies?
- How much do you order?
- How far in advance do you need to place your order?
- Do you get special price breaks?
- Do you have an account with your vendor that others can use to order products on your behalf?

## Production Processes

- What materials are used? How many?
- What tools and equipment are needed?
- If you are assembling a product, what goes into each product? Is there a certain order? Are there certain color combinations, quantities, or measurements?
- Is there a template or sample to refer to?
- How many should you make?
- How many should you always have on hand?
- How and where do you store your finished products?

## Shipping and Delivery Processes

- What methods do you use to ship?
- How much do you charge for shipping and handling?

## RIGHT-BRAIN ENTREPRENEUR SPOTLIGHT

 Multimedia artist Desiree Habicht produces designs she licenses for use on fabrics and other products. As part of her Smooth Sailing Systems, Desiree follows the same steps each time she develops quilt patterns. Not only does repeating what works make her more efficient, but it also ensures high quality in her final product. Her procedures cover everything from sketching an initial concept, to creating a prototype of the design, to market testing at trade shows before investing in a larger, more cost-effective print run. She also brings in cohorts to test and edit the pattern measurements and instructions and, at key decision points, determines whether to move forward with a final design.

Desiree explains how her repeatable moola-making methods have benefited her: "I have patterns that have been printed several times, and which have been on the market for more than ten years. I found that when they are popular they never seem to get old; new customers are being made every day who have not seen the patterns at all. Although I need to continually show new things, the old ones still keep selling."

- Do you ship internation-
  ally?
- How often do you ship?
  How soon after an order
  is placed do you ship the
  items?
- What type of shipping
  and packing supplies are
  needed, and where do you order them?
- Does a third party handle shipping or delivery for you? Do
  they also manage inventory and customer support regard-
  ing orders?
- Are your goods perishable? Do you need to deliver them
  locally the same day?

## Marketing and Brand Processes

- Do you have a brand style guide? Are there certain fonts and
  colors that should be used?
- What are the standard sizes for images on your website? Do
  you have a naming convention and preferred file type?
- Do you have templates for things like your newsletters and
  email announcements? Who writes and sends each issue of
  the newsletter? How often does that happen?
- Do you have templates for your love letters, web pages, or blog
  posts? Who updates those? How often does that happen?
- Do you have a promotional, social-media, or editorial calendar? Who manages it? How far in advance do you need to
  know what will go into the calendar?

## Reporting Processes

- Do you have a system that lets you easily look up stats such
  as email open rates, number of people on your list(s), and
  rate of conversion from connection to customer?
- Do you have systems by which you can easily find out how
  much you've sold in a day, month, quarter, or year; who

your repeat customers are; how many upgrades you've sold; or which are your bestselling products?

- How do you track your moola-in and moola-out? How often do you track it?

## Backup and Contingency Plans

- What are your backup procedures to prevent the loss of important information?
- What happens if your regular process fails or your systems are down?
- Who is your backup if you are not available? Who is your backup's backup?

## RIGHT-BRAIN ENTREPRENEUR SPOTLIGHT

Veteran business owner Patty Donahue founded her retail store, Image Awards, Engraving and Creative Keepsakes, in 1994 in Geneva, Illinois. Her core message is about helping people make meaningful and lasting impressions through her engraved corporate awards, trophies, signage, and gifts.

Patty's basic Smooth Sailing Systems include QuickBooks to manage her finances, FileMaker for invoicing customers, and Constant Contact to send out her monthly newsletter. Another crucial Smooth Sailing System is her store policy. Since her pieces are personalized, she doesn't offer refunds or store credit unless there's an error on her part. Her policy also covers deposits and what happens when she's personalizing an item owned by the customer.

Patty speaks from years of experience when she says, "These decisions are best made at the beginning. Post your policy in your store. Verbalize your policy to your clients. Make sure they understand. If you feel it's necessary, have them initial a form saying they accept your policy — convey to them a lighthearted 'We're great, but we're not perfect' message. Just sound human. After all, our customers are human, too, and they understand and even appreciate that you've taken these things into consideration. It actually builds trust."

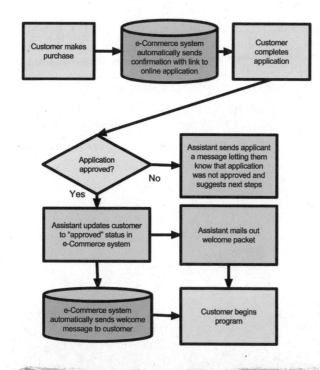

Visual process maps transform a complex set of steps and decision points into a user-friendly guide. Color-code various shapes to represent certain tools, types of actions, or who is responsible for the task.

## The Temptation of Technology and Tools

Please, don't spend all your time trying to find the perfect tool. That's really just another great procrastination technique. It's unlikely you'll find a system that will meet all your needs. Be clear about your priorities and minimum requirements, use the most basic tool to meet those needs, and allow yourself to grow into your Smooth Sailing Systems. When you're ready to look at tools, check in with your cohorts, professional groups, or social media network for recommendations.

For example, you may be smitten with a slick, new (and pricey) online project-planning tool with all the bells

### LEFT-BRAIN CHILL PILL

Overwhelmed by all the decisions you need to make in your business? With documented processes, the decisions can be spelled out for you. Instead of worrying about each situation, you can turn to your record of procedures and repeat what worked before.

and whistles, while, as a solo act, you really could get by with a spread-sheet or maybe even handwritten notes on a whiteboard. Eventually you might invest in a more robust or integrated infrastructure. Perhaps your manual process will become too time-consuming. Or the cost of using the separate tools you've pieced together for things like email marketing and e-commerce now exceeds the price of a higher-end system that handles both. When you do reach a certain level of volume and complexity in your business, integrated systems and infrastructure make sense and can help you accelerate your growth even more.

If you're feeling especially adventurous and creative, get inspired by the wall-sized "aspen grove" magnetic plan made by Amy Christensen, owner of Expand Outdoors. This visual helps her get a handle on all the moving pieces of her business operations, since the various elements are easy to move around and update as her priorities shift. Photos © Rebecca Stumpf.

If you have a team, make sure you have procedures and tools to help everyone get on the same page. For example, my assistant and I have a standing hour-long weekly meeting by phone. We use a shared Google document to list our agenda items for the call, and we use that to track any previous action items as well. In our shared Google calendar, my assistant makes note of regularly scheduled tasks, reminders, communications, travel dates, and deadlines. We also have a shared document with answers to frequently asked questions, and my assistant can reference that when responding to customer inquiries. You may decide to manage team communications via email or Google Docs, or you may opt for a collaborative project management tool such as Basecamp or Smartsheet.

Roughly once a quarter, we set aside time for a longer meeting in person so we can look at

**RIGHT-BRAIN BOOSTER**

Take time to reflect. Your Smooth Sailing Systems may include pausing to note what's working or not working, so that you can continuously improve and innovate. Download the Stop, Start, Continue and the Left-Brain/Right-Brain Assessments illustrated play sheets to use during quarterly reviews at www.rightbrain businessplan.com/rbbiz.

the next three to six months on the sticky-note project plan. We figure out how the various offers and launches feed into each other, and we map out our schedule. For example, are there too many things going on at once? Do we have enough time to market something before launching it? Are there months when no moola is coming in, when we're planning to focus on developing something and need a sale or some other easy moola-making method to fill in the gap? For more ideas on mapping out a quarter or year, refer to chapter 6; and for tips on building your team, see chapter 8.

- Identify your business-critical processes.
- Write your honey-do list(s).
- For right-brained flair, enhance your documentation with color and images.

## LEFT-BRAIN CHECKLIST

Your left brain appreciates keeping track of the steps you've taken toward your sustained success.

- ❏ I have easily accessible and updatable documented processes for my most business-critical activities.
- ❏ I have the basic systems, tools, and infrastructure in place to meet the needs of my business.
- ❏ I have shared my Smooth Sailing Systems with my team so that we are all on the same page and they know how to perform their tasks.
- ❏ I am repeating what works and making continuous improvements so I can reap the rewards.

# Embracing Ease

## Creating Calm amid the Chaos of Life

First off, yay to you for putting in the time and energy to build your business in a way that works for you. You've done a lot of work to get this far. At the beginning of this book, we talked about sustained success. That means success on your terms over the long haul. You don't want the result of all your efforts to be no more than a flash in the pan. You want staying power. This means ensuring that you have the stamina to stick around and continue to share your gifts profitably and whole-heartedly.

### The Importance of the Pause

Maybe you've pushed hard to reach a certain level of success, and you know you can't keep up that pace forever. You worry, though, that if you pause even for a second you're going to miss out on something really important. Your "competition" will launch some fantastic product before you can do it, or you'll lose out on a perfect new client or project, or you'll fall even further behind on your never-ending to-do list, or your opportunities for profitable partnerships will wither on the vine. Sound familiar? I've felt that way myself, and I've heard similar concerns from other overachievers and busybodies.

Well, even though it may not seem businesslike, sometimes resting and being gentle with yourself is exactly what's needed to take you to your next level of success. Taking time out clears your head and creates the space necessary for you to listen to your inner wisdom. And by connecting with that inner wisdom, you'll make more strategic decisions that support the overall health of your business, instead of killing yourself by constantly reacting to everyday fires.

As Count Rugen said in one of my favorite movies, *The Princess Bride*: "Get some rest. If you haven't got your health, then you haven't got anything."

You are head honcho of your creative work, which means *you* are your business. When you take care of yourself, you take care of your business, and in turn you can take better care of your customers. See, it's a virtuous circle. That's why we have a whole chapter dedicated to embracing ease. Heck, even though it's not full of left-brain, nitty-gritty business tactics, it may be the most important chapter for sustaining your long-term success.

In other words, take this section to heart.

If you don't tend to your well-being, you're bound to run into problems. This is especially important if you're an overachiever or you're feeling overwhelmed or overworked. Remember, you are your own boss, and one of the joys of working for yourself is that you get to call the shots. So make sure that taking care of yourself is at the top of the agenda.

## LEFT-BRAIN CHILL PILL

Put things in perspective. Whether "good" or "bad" things happen, stress is associated with important life events, and these take up your mind space and your energy. To see how the events in your own life may be contributing to your stress levels, do an Internet search on the Holmes-Rahe stress scale and do the assessment. You may be surprised to realize how much you've been trying to cope with. So, please, go easy on yourself.

## Life Happens

Let's face it: no matter how much we plan or desperately try to control everything, business (and life) gets messy. That's why creating calm amid the chaos is essential for riding the ups and downs of business and life.

During the months when I was working on this book, my life was especially chaotic. While I was still in recovery mode following one of my biggest launches of the year, my husband got into a bicycle accident and had to have surgery. I had been struggling with my own health issues, including chronic pain and fatigue, for quite some time already. We were both stressed out about increased crime in our neighborhood, so we decided to sell our house, which meant putting most of our belongings in storage and moving to San Francisco temporarily. Fortunately, within a few days of closing on our old house, our offer on a new one was accepted. Then we spent the next couple of months getting the place fixed up before we moved in. And on top of all that, my dad took a bad fall that sent him to the hospital for three weeks, so I made a couple of trips to Southern California to help my family. All this is to say that I get it — life happens! And sometimes when it rains it pours. I'm happy to report that my husband, my dad, and I are all doing better now. Whew!

Even in the midst of what felt like an unusual amount of upheaval, I had my best first and second quarters to date, bringing in during a six-month period nearly what I had made during the full year before. I attribute that to having created a solid foundation for my business, using what I've covered so far in this book, and practicing the embracing-ease strategies I share in this chapter.

## The Five Embracing-Ease Strategies for Sustained Success

Here are five strategies that will help you embrace ease in your business:

- *Simplicity* — What's the easiest thing to do?

- *Spaciousness* — What can you let go of?
- *Self-care* — What will refuel you?
- *Support* — Who can you ask for help? This is discussed in chapter 8.
- *Systems* — What processes or tools can you put in place to make things go more smoothly? This is discussed in chapter 9.

In this chapter we'll explore the first three strategies so you can learn to integrate them into your life and business. They are all interrelated, so focusing on one area can help bring more ease in another. Since the final two strategies are covered in some depth in chapters 8 and 9, respectively, you can refer to those chapters for more detail.

Use the Embracing Ease play sheet to help implement the five strategies. Refer to the legend at the bottom of the play sheet for the questions to consider, and write your answers in the respective colored areas.

## Simplicity

Do you feel like you need to work really, really hard in order to make things count? That success comes only with lots of blood, sweat, and tears, elbow grease, and dues-paying? If your work is easy, do you feel like you're cheating, you're lazy, or you're somehow getting away with something? Many overachievers get trapped into thinking that something is significant or successful only when it's difficult to accomplish.

I am amazed at how often I make things harder and more complicated than they are. Perhaps it comes from being conditioned to prove that I'm smart or clever — and to believe that the more complex something is, the more it demonstrates how much I know. The truth is, it usually takes more know-how to come up with a simple and elegant solution. So don't work harder. Find the path of least resistance and gain momentum.

## RIGHT-BRAIN REFLECTION

Imagine for a moment that things are simple, easy. That you're able to run your business gracefully and still have energy to spare. Allow yourself to breathe and contemplate that. If you could experience such ease in your work, what would open up for you? Take a moment to journal your thoughts.

# Embracing Ease

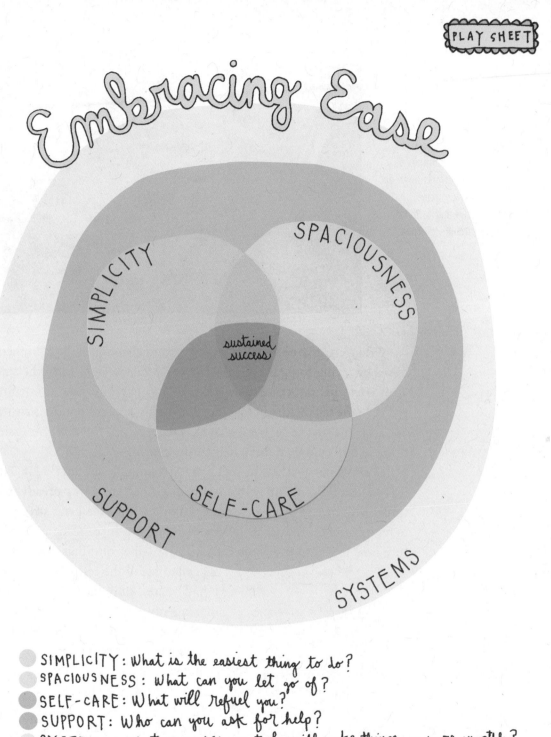

SPACIOUSNESS

SIMPLICITY

sustained success

SELF-CARE

SUPPORT

SYSTEMS

SIMPLICITY: What is the easiest thing to do?

SPACIOUSNESS: What can you let go of?

SELF-CARE: What will refuel you?

SUPPORT: Who can you ask for help?

SYSTEMS: What processes or tools will make things go more smoothly?

Yoga teacher and life coach Sharon Tessandori embraces ease by giving herself permission to do her work in an environment that feeds her creative spirit. Photo credit: Retta Ritchie-Holbrook.

Often, creative entrepreneurs with grand visions get ahead of themselves by trying to figure out the whole enchilada right from the start. They overwhelm themselves while trying to map out how all the little pieces of the big picture fit together. Inevitably, analysis paralysis ensues.

Stop making it so complicated. Ask yourself, "What's the easiest thing to do?" and then do it. Keep it simple.

In 2008, my goal was to create my first tangible product, a kit. That was an idea I'd come up with a few years earlier, and I was already frustrated with myself for having done nothing with it yet. I was struggling to figure out how to source the materials and produce the kit and wasn't sure how to brand it or how it fit with my other offerings. I was overwhelmed by all the research I thought I had to do, and the numbers were making my head spin. After months of getting nowhere, I needed a quick win. I knew that completing something would get me unstuck.

I asked myself, what do I have that is simple and easy and could be put together quickly? The answer popped up as if it had been there all along. I

## LEFT-BRAIN CHILL PILL

Having trouble deciding what would be the easiest thing to do? Leave it to chance: flip a coin. Or write your choices on slips of paper and pull one out of a hat. Eliminate the hemming and hawing and get yourself going.

would do a short, nine-page illustrated e-book with the help of my dear friend Kate. I gave Kate my text and talked her through my ideas for images. We had one round of design, and within a month I was selling my first e-book. That gave me the confidence needed to finish my other project. And some of the things I learned from producing the e-book helped me create and sell that first kit.

By asking myself what would be easiest, I gave myself permission to go for a quick win, and from there I built momentum. That little nine-page e-book was the unexpected and humble start of the Right-Brain Business Plan arm of my business.

On the cover of my 2013 Right-Brain Business Plan, I placed a Thoreau quote to remind me to keep things simple: "Simplify. Simplify."

## Spaciousness

The second strategy for embracing ease is spaciousness. Ask yourself, "What can I let go of?"

Are you stressed out because you're trying to do too much? You have permission to do what works best for you. If you're overwhelmed because you're trying out every suggestion in this book and in all the other books and blogs you've been reading, give yourself a break. The most helpful thing to do is to focus on a few key things. The rest you can let go.

Creative entrepreneurs frequently tell me how exhausted they feel while managing their mile-long to-do lists. When you did the Entrepreneurial Ecosystem exercise at the beginning of the book, did you list chores that were really just busywork, items that currently are not getting you the results you want? Let them go. Just because something works for someone else, that doesn't mean you must do things exactly the same way.

Heart-centered, generous, creative souls tend to give, give, give to other people. But just because people request something from you, that doesn't mean you have to say yes to everything. Consider where you are in your life or business right now, and use your body and intuition as a barometer. If something you think you should do doesn't feel completely right for you, then let it go.

Create white space on your calendar. This scheduled "pause button" will enhance your creativity and replenish your reserves (see more on that in the self-care strategy, which I'll get to in a minute). And it promotes the mental clarity needed to develop new work for making moola later. Strategic thinking, big-picture thinking, requires energy and a frame of mind unlike those needed for administrative tasks, day-to-day operations, and the work of serving your clients.

To create spaciousness in your life, try a few of these suggestions:

- Be willing to say no, even when it scares you.
- Dedicate at least a couple of hours a week to focusing on big-picture and moola-later activities.
- Schedule a half or full day at least once a quarter to reflect on your progress.
- Take time off throughout the year. Unplug. Go on a vacation or retreat. Schedule these mental-health days ahead of time so you can plan your launches and work around them. And be open to going on spontaneous trips and adventures, because sometimes you need a break NOW.
- Build in some recovery time after launches, after intensive work periods, and after trips. This could mean blocking off a few days on your calendar following a big event so you can

decompress, or simply blocking off half an hour in between client meetings so you can catch your breath.

- Rest in advance. Don't wait until you've pushed through a deadline; take care of yourself during your busiest times. That way you'll have the energy you need to carry you past the finish line.

I created this "Be Gentle with Yourself" card to remind myself to slow down. When I feel rushed or overwhelmed, a glance at it helps me embrace ease and breathe more deeply.

## Knowing When to Walk Away

Since we're discussing spaciousness and what to let go of, it's worth asking, "When is it the right time to walk away from a piece of your business or from your company altogether?" If you're considering closing up shop, don't think of it as a failure. Instead, explore the ways that you may be able to evolve what you were doing into something else that works better for you.

When I had a corporate job and was coaching on the side, I also had a fledgling bookbinding business using fine Japanese papers. While I loved being crafty and making beautiful photo albums and wish boxes, I detested schlepping my stuff to art shows. I also discovered that I didn't enjoy doing custom work. I wasn't happy with some of the commissioned work I did, because the colors and patterns I was asked to use on those pieces were not combinations I would have put together. It was great that the customers were happy with their orders, but I didn't like being dissatisfied with my work. That took the joy out of the creative process.

Since I was tracking the left-brain details of my business ventures, I could see that the coaching side of the business was bringing in more money, with fewer expenses, than the handmade art. And I was enjoying the coaching more. I didn't want to lose the artistic aspect of what I was doing, though, so by trial and error I found a way to be creative in my business. Instead of making pieces by hand, I've developed products and processes, in a coaching context, that let people create their own meaningful artwork.

## RIGHT-BRAIN REFLECTION

Take a moment to think about times in your life when you've felt the most at ease, peaceful, and energized. What did you do (or not do) to create that feeling for yourself? Are there certain things you know you must do to nourish your well-being and creative spirit? What are those?

When your work is no longer working for you, your business is not sustainable. Here are some indicators to watch for:

- You're not happy.
- You no longer enjoy doing the work.
- You're not bringing in enough money.
- Your expenses are too high.
- Your work takes up too much time and energy.
- Your work requires too many resources or resources you're not able or willing to invest in it.
- You're not attracting the customers you want to work with.
- Your work no longer aligns with your vision and values.

If you can imagine no longer operating your business, or a part of your business, and this actually feels like a huge relief, pay attention to that clue. Letting go can be challenging, but when you have the courage to do it, new doors inevitably will open. When you walk through them, you'll find a new way to align what you do with your vision and values.

## Self-Care

Self-care, the third strategy in embracing ease, is not necessarily about pampering yourself or living a life of luxury (although those can certainly be part of self-care if you choose). I'm talking about energy management and nourishing your creative spirit.

Expressing your gratitude is a wonderful act of self-care. Cass Mullane of Prosper Creatively acknowledges the things she's thankful for by noting them on slips of paper and dropping them into in her "Cool Stuff Jar." At the end of the year, she reviews the jar's contents to celebrate her accomplishments and renew her appreciation.

## RIGHT-BRAIN BOOSTER

Release your emotions. Sometimes you just gotta let yourself have a big old cry when you're happy, sad, or anything in between. Acknowledging your feelings in the moment helps you tend to your needs and opens up a deep well of creativity.

Ask yourself, "What will refuel me?" Self-care is different for everyone, which is why you'll want to check in with yourself to see what you need.

When you don't engage in self-care, what happens and how do you feel? Do you let frustrations build up until you explode? Do you feel resentful? Sluggish? Depressed? Angry? Write down the words that describe what you feel when you've reached the end of your rope. It's important to be aware of the early warning signs, so you can make sure you don't get to that point.

When you feel you simply have no time to take care of yourself, that is absolutely the most important time for self-care. Please don't ignore this. Even if you're on a tight deadline or you're experiencing a particularly hectic period in your life, find ways to take care of yourself. You may not be able to enjoy a three-hour hike in the woods, but I bet you can spare ten minutes to walk around the block. Besides, it will do wonders for clearing your head and giving you a fresh perspective — probably just the thing you need to make it through the day.

It took me a while to understand my creative cycles and flow, but I eventually realized that I do better when I have longer periods of quiet time. So, in 2008, I began practicing what I call self-care Fridays — days that I spend just on myself. On these days I keep my calendar clear of calls and meetings (except for appointments with my hairstylist, massage therapist, the local nail shop, my inner muse, or dear friends). I take quiet time to just be. It needn't take up the entire day; knowing that I have even a few hours of white space helps me recharge. When I don't gift myself with this weekly miniretreat, I get cranky and resentful. And when I allow myself to indulge in some breathing space, I relax, enjoy, and even get inspired!

Just because I have a day dedicated to self-care doesn't mean I put off all self-care time until Friday. I still find small moments each day to draw from my self-care catalog. You can create your own in the following exercise.

## EXERCISE
## Create Your Own Self-Care Catalog

What you'll need:

- A piece of paper or your journal
- Markers
- Magazines or catalogs (optional)
- Scissors (optional)
- Glue stick (optional)
- A jar or box (optional)

When you're feeling depleted, you won't want to use your impaired decision-making ability to figure out what will help you spring back. To make things easy on yourself, create a self-care catalog to choose from. That way you don't have to think about it.

Simply make an entertaining and colorful list of all your favorite self-care activities. You can also use magazine clippings to enhance your self-care catalog. Or surprise yourself with a self-care treat: Write each self-care item on a slip of paper and place it in a pretty jar or box. When you need to refuel, pull a slip out of the jar at random and enjoy!

My self-care catalog reminds me of some of my favorite ways to take care of myself.

As you can see in the image from my self-care catalog, my favorite self-care activities are mainly simple, inexpensive pleasures that I can easily fit into the middle of the day. Some require a bit more planning or investment, but the majority are great, impromptu, no-cost pick-me-ups that I can turn to as needed. I'm also very much a homebody and an introvert, and my self-care catalog reflects that. You're uniquely you, so your self-care catalog may include things like going on a road trip with friends, dancing at a club, or playing ultimate Frisbee. Your list will be made up of whatever reenergizes you, so refer back to what you jotted down in this section's Right-Brain Reflection.

## RIGHT-BRAIN BOOSTER

Get enough sleep each night. When you're well rested, you're more creative, so know how much sleep you need and make sure you give that to yourself. And let yourself indulge in power naps every once in a while, too!

Some of the things in your self-care catalog may require money. Just remember that part of the reason you're in business for yourself is to be able to enjoy the things you love to do. Go back to the work you did in chapter 7 and make sure you took these things into account when you dreamed up your moola goals. For example, my friend Kate is a mom who loves yoga. Even though her weekly yoga class costs a lot when she factors in hiring a babysitter, she says that self-care is worth the investment.

Massage is one of the top items in my self-care catalog. It can be pricey, but I got creative. A few years ago, rather than waiting until I was in desperate need of a long massage, I started getting ten- or fifteen-minute chair massages at a local grocery store. It was a nice little treat that helped keep my stress levels down and didn't cost a fortune. Recently I decided to invest in a massage membership, and now I can get more frequent massages. It makes me happy.

## RIGHT-BRAIN ENTREPRENEUR SPOTLIGHT

Professional organizer Beth DeZiel of Lasso shares some of her ingredients for sustained success:

Surrounding myself with people who believe in me and support me no matter what.

Learning to value myself and my time above all else. This is the surest way for me to get into an energetic groove with my business and experience the pure joy of sharing my gifts with the world.

Immersing myself in Systems 101: creating rituals to start my day, streamlining the way I approach my work, developing a daily schedule, and purging from my life the people, habits, and beliefs that no longer serve me.

## Make Your Schedule Work for You

Isn't it funny how much time people spend pondering, researching, and trying out the latest time-management techniques? Not to mention the time they waste berating themselves for not being productive. Ha, I've been there, too! That's why I've made this section on time management as brief as possible.

I use a few simple practices that help me make the most of my time. First, I acknowledge my energy levels. For example, I know that I don't function well before ten in the morning, so I rarely schedule anything that requires me to sound coherent before then. Know when you're most creative and productive, and manage your days accordingly. I also know that as an introvert I need uninterrupted, inward-focused time to dive deeply into things like product development, writing, and moola-later activities. So, while working I eliminate distractions by turning off my Wi-Fi and putting my phone in airplane mode. I listen to thirty-to-sixty-minute playlists to help me settle into and time my activity, and I usually work for much longer stints once I get in my groove.

**ACTION ACCELERATOR**

Open up your calendar right now and block off at least two hours on one day this week that will be time just for you. On that day savor something from your self-care catalog.

Rather than hold myself to a rigid, left-brain, hour-by-hour daily schedule, I prefer blocking off time for my activities according to my inward and outward energy. Here's an example of how a typical week flows for me:

- *Monday:* I take client calls, handle some administrative and business-building tasks, and meet with my assistant to plan out the week.
- *Tuesday:* I block off time for my own projects, such as writing, developing new products or programs, business development, or working with my own coach.
- *Wednesday:* I take client calls, lead group calls for my programs, and do any guest interviews.
- *Thursday:* I focus on my own projects (similar to Tuesday).
- *Friday:* I practice self-care.

Make up your own calendar in a way that acknowledges your energy flow.

## Reserves and Resilience: You're Raring to Go!

The more your business grows, the more important it is for you to embrace ease. It will make the difference between just getting by and enjoying sustainable success. Simplicity, spaciousness, and self-care create a valuable reserve of creative energy that keeps you ahead of the game and resilient in the face of challenges. And the more you expand your reach and increase your visibility, the more you'll attract invitations, prospects, and potential partners. You want to be ready to say yes to your next big break, not break down from exhaustion. Embracing ease gives you the capacity to both jump at unexpected opportunities and steadily cultivate your company over time.

Even though it may feel counterintuitive at times, pressing that precious pause button can be the best thing you do for your business.

## Recap of Activities

- Look up the Holmes-Rahe stress scale to see how events in your life may be affecting your health.
- Create your own self-care catalog.
- Schedule your activities in time blocks that accommodate your energetic flow.
- Block off at least two hours this week to create time just for you.

 **LEFT-BRAIN CHECKLIST**

Your left brain appreciates keeping track of the steps you've taken toward your sustained success.

- ❏ I choose what's simple and easy.
- ❏ I let go of things that aren't working or that no longer serve me.
- ❏ I practice self-care regularly.
- ❏ I ask my circle of support for help.
- ❏ I have my Smooth Sailing Systems in place.

# Conclusion

Alas, my right-brained friend, we've come to the end of our journey together in this book. But more important, your own journey toward sustainable success will continue with each action you take.

Take a moment and reflect on how you defined success at the beginning of this book. What does sustainable success mean to you now? Has your perspective of success changed? And how are you already successful?

Revisit your Entrepreneurial Ecosystem assessment and your Sustainable Success Survey monthly or quarterly to stay mindful of your company's health, and make adjustments along the way.

Remember that when you take consistent, concrete steps forward from a place of passion, purpose, and service, you can make a meaningful and positive difference. From that sweet spot the money will flow.

The path to success may come with twists and turns, but as a right-brainer you instinctively know how to ride the creative process that comes with your business.

On your journey as a right-brain entrepreneur, remember:

- Be patient and loving with yourself and know that each small step you take counts big time. Remain inspired and act.
- The more you put yourself and your work out there, the more you learn. And the more you learn, the more you can grow your business.
- Your right people need what you have to offer, and you're just the right person to help them. Whether you strive to leave a lasting legacy, or you simply want to make your modest mark, honor your commitment to making a difference by continuing to share your special gifts with the world.
- Be open to receiving the abundance you deserve.
- Celebrate, enjoy, and invest in yourself. Taking care of yourself is taking care of your business.
- Making your ideas real will give you the confidence, experience, and savvy to keep on manifesting more meaningful magic. Repeat what works. Keep on spreading your magic.
- Here's to your continued success and creative flow!

♥, jenn

# Optional *Right-Brain Business Plan Exercises to Reference*

I f you've already completed some of the exercises from my first book, *The Right-Brain Business Plan*, feel free to reference your previous work as you go through this book, *Building Your Business the Right-Brain Way*. Your visual plan may help you gain new or deeper insights into your business as you go through this process.

And please, don't worry if you haven't read *The Right-Brain Business Plan*. You're not required to do those exercises first before diving into this book. On the next page, I've provided references to previous exercises, simply to encourage further insight.

## Optional *Right-Brain Business Plan* Exercises to Reference

| For these chapters in *Building Your Business the Right-Brain Way*... | you can reference the following exercises or play sheets from *The Right-Brain Business Plan*[*] |
| --- | --- |
| Chapter 2. Tending Your Entrepreneurial Ecosystem | • Dream Big with the Big-Vision Visualization (pages 33–36)<br>• Flip and Clip to Start Making Your Big-Vision Collage (pages 38–41)<br>• Create a Card Deck of Your Values (pages 43–45)<br>• Pen Your Passion and Purpose Proclamation (pages 46–47)<br>• Make Your Moola Map (pages 106–10)<br>• Summing It All Up in Your Managing the Moola Plan (pages 119–20) |
| Chapter 3. Taking a Stand and Making an Impact | • Flip and Clip to Start Making Your Big-Vision Collage (pages 38–41)<br>• Pen Your Passion and Purpose Proclamation (pages 46–47)<br>• Create a Business Self-Portrait (pages 66–68) |
| Chapter 4. Attracting, Engaging, and Learning from Your Right Peeps | • Collage Your Perfect Customer Portraits (pages 79–81)<br>• Write Character Sketches of Your Perfect Customers (pages 82–84)<br>• Role-Play with a Friend (pages 84–85) |
| Chapter 5. Packaging Your Gifts and Crafting Your Offer | • Flip and Clip to Start Making Your Big-Vision Collage (pages 38–41)<br>• Pen Your Passion and Purpose Proclamation (pages 46–47)<br>• The Business Landscape play sheet (pages 50–51)<br>• Create a Business Self-Portrait (pages 66–68) |
| Chapter 6. Let's Do Launch | • The Getting the Word Out Play Sheet (pages 93–96) |
| Chapter 7. Making More Moola | • Make Your Moola Map (pages 106–10)<br>• The Rid the Red, Grow the Green, Spreadsheet (pages 114–15)<br>• Summing It All Up in Your Managing the Moola Plan (pages 119–20) |
| Chapter 8. In Good Company | • Make a Helping-Hands Wish List (page 125)<br>• Make a Creative Cohorts Visual Map — the Creative Cohorts play sheet (pages 140–42) |
| Chapter 9. Smooth Sailing Systems | • The Operational Plan (pages 179–80) |
| Chapter 10. Embracing Ease | • Right-Brain Booster: Keep a "kudos and feel-good" folder (page 185) |

[*]  NOTE: I've included page numbers for the exercises in *The Right-Brain Business Plan*, but if you have an electronic book you can locate the exercise using the exercise title as keywords in a search.

# Resources

For selected chapters, I've highlighted a handful of resources and tools to help you run your business. Visit www.rightbrainbusiness plan.com/rbbiz for other suggested links.

## Marketing/Newsletter Systems (Chapter 4)

www.mailchimp.com
www.aweber.com
www.infusionsoft.com (integrated with e-commerce)
www.1shoppingcart.com (integrated with e-commerce)

## Smartphone Photography and Graphic Tools (Chapter 4)

www.instagram.com
www.abeautifulmess.com/a-beautiful-mess-app (for adding graphics and text to your photos)
www.madewithover.com (for adding text to your photos)
www.picmonkey.com (free online photo editor)

## Tools for Surveying Customers or Collecting Feedback (Chapter 4)

www.wufoo.com
www.surveymonkey.com
drive.google.com (Google Forms)

## Tools and Resources for Creating Courses
## or Information Products (Chapter 5)

www.livestream.com (for live video streaming and chat)

www.vimeo.com (for video storage and streaming)

www.rezuku.com (for hosting e-courses)

www.freeconferencepro.com (for hosting and recording conference calls)

## E-Commerce Systems (Chapters 6 and 7)

www.e-junkie.com

www.shopify.com

www.1shoppingcart.com

www.infusionsoft.com

## Easy Ways to Get Paid (Chapter 7)

www.paypal.com

www.squareup.com

## Bookkeeping (Chapter 7)

www.quickbooks.com

bookkeeping.godaddy.com

www.freshbooks.com

## File Sharing and Collaboration Tools (Chapters 8 and 9)

www.dropbox.com

drive.google.com (for Google Docs and Google Spreadsheets)

www.basecamp.com

www.smartsheet.com

## Meeting and Appointment Scheduling Systems (Chapter 9)

www.bookfresh.com

www.timetrade.com

www.scheduleonce.com

calendar.google.com

## Office and Art Supplies

Paper Source, for beautifully designed wall calendars (my favorite is the Academic Great Big Wall Calendar), fancy sticky notes, washi tape, markers and pens, accordion-book kits, paper, envelopes, and cards. Online store (www.paper-source.com) and locations across the United States.

Levenger, for a few of my favorite note-taking tools, including Circa notebooks (there's a Right-Brain Business Plan one!), Special Request Storyboard sheets, Note Card Bleachers (great for organizing index cards), and the Oasis Shaded Annotation Concept Pads (great for organizing sticky notes). Online store (www.levenger.com) and select retail locations across the United States.

## Books

Since I'd prefer that you take action in the real world rather than bury your head in more books, I've kept my reading recommendations to five favorites that pack a punch.

*The $100 Startup*, by Chris Guillebeau
*Book Yourself Solid ILLUSTRATED*, by Michael Port
*The Fire Starter Sessions*, by Danielle LaPorte
*Steal Like an Artist*, by Austin Kleon
*To Sell Is Human*, by Daniel Pink

# Featured Right-Brain Entrepreneurs

Jackie Blain
www.jackieblain.com

Ho'omalamalama Brown
Manaia Design and Production
www.hoomalamalama.com

Laura Burns
Laura Burns Consulting
www.lauraburnsconsulting.com

Amy Christensen
Expand Outdoors
www.expandoutdoors.com

Mary K. Clark
Storyteller, writer, and creativity and play
facilitator
www.marykclark.com

Caitlin Colling
Image consultant and wardrobe stylist
www.collingimage.com

Amy A. Crawley
www.amyacrawley.com

Beth DeZiel
Lasso, LLC, modern-day wrangler of time
and space
www.lassollc.com

Patty Donahue
Image Awards, Engraving & Creative
Keepsakes, Inc.
www.ImageAwards.net

Monica Garcia
Divine Light Coaching
www.divinelightcoaching.com

Melissa Gazzaneo
Reskü
www.reskugear.com

Kiala Givehand
Giving Hands Creative
www.kialagivehand.com

Desiree Habicht
Desiree's Designs Studios
www.desireesdesigns.com

Tiffany Han, CPCC
Tiffany Han Coaching
www.tiffanyhan.com

Jill McCoy
Visual Jill
www.visualjill.com

Vivienne McMaster
Be Your Own Beloved workshops
www.beyourownbeloved.com

Susan Stott Miller, PhD, LPCS
Miller Counseling Services, PC
Lighted Path® Coaching
www.lightedpathcoaching.org

Cass Mullane
Prosper Creatively, LLC
www.prospercreatively.com

Brighid O'Shaughnessy
Erasing the Distance
www.erasingthedistance.org

Sheila Pai
A Living Family
Parenting, relationship, and life coaching
www.sheilapai.com

Cynthia Patton
Writer, editor, advocate, speaker,
    special needs attorney, and autism mom
Founder, Autism A to Z
www.cynthiajpatton.com

Mari Pfeiffer
Writer and web designer
www.maripfeiffer.com

Nicole Piar
Illustrator and surface designer
www.ghostkitten.com

Kate Prentiss
Art director, illustrator, and graphic designer
www.kateprentiss.com

Kerri Richardson
Intuitive life and business strategist
www.kerririchardson.com

Elle Roberts
The Creative Business Co.
www.creativebusinessco.com

Helene Rose
Be Brilliant Network
www.bebrilliantnetwork.com

Lou Shackleton
The You Can Hub
www.theyoucanhub.org.uk

Bindi Shah
Anamaya
www.anamaya.net

Shari Sherman
Shari Sherman! Art and Inspiration
www.sharisherman.com

Virginia Simpson-Magruder
Kentucky Girl Designs
www.kentuckygirldesigns.com

Tammi Spruill
Fruition
www.fruitioncreativestudio.com

Sarah Stevenson
Redlinedesign
www.sarahgstevenson.com

Rebecca Stumpf
Editorial and commercial photographer
www.rebeccastumpf.com

Sharon Tessandori
Barefootworks
www.barefootworks.com

Mary Maru Wright
Mary Maru Design
www.marymaru.com

Jen Young
Spitfire Fitness Arts
www.spitfirefitnessarts.wordpress.com

# Acknowledgments

Surrounding yourself with awesome people is one of the keys to sustainable success. I'm grateful to be surrounded by the following amazing folks, who I'd especially like to thank for helping to make this book possible:

My husband and soul mate, Brian Ng, for believing in me and this book, for shooting artwork, and for handling all the new house stuff while I was on deadline.

The best-ever creative cohort/friend and my other soul mate, Kate Prentiss, for making collaboration so easy, for outdoing herself yet again with the incredible illustrations in this book, and for cooking up the cover concept.

My amazing friend and assistant Stefanie Renée, who came in and saved the day when she said YES to joining the team.

My business mentor and sister-from-another-mother, Andrea J. Lee, for helping me create sustainable success and for always holding a bigger vision for me.

My wonderful editor, Georgia Hughes, and the team at New World Library, including Monique Muhlenkamp, Tracy Cunningham, Tona Pearce Myers, Ami Parkerson, Munro Magruder, Kristen Cashman, Jonathan Wichmann, Kim Corbin, and Marc Allen, for all their hard work. Plus, my copyeditor, Bonita Hurd, for polishing up the manuscript.

Michael Port for enthusiastically agreeing to write the foreword for this book and for being such an inspiring thought-leader.

Janet Goldstein and Elizabeth Marshall for their invaluable advice and publishing-industry expertise.

My dear friend Hannah Lynde Wittman for saying just the right words to me at just the right times and for being the most awesome hiking buddy.

My Nurture Huddle — Leah Piken Kolidas, Jessie Marianiello, and Darlene Kreutzer — for all the love, laughter, and tears we've shared through the years.

My leadership tribe mates — Lisa Anderson, Tina de Meeus, Fiona Sturrock, Rebecca Hourston, and Brighid O'Shaughnessy — for more than a decade of calling me forth.

Amy Christensen, Kiala Givehand, Tiffany Han, and Vivienne McMaster for providing such helpful feedback on the draft manuscript and for their encouragement and support.

All the featured right-brain entrepreneurs in this book for sharing their stories and artwork.

My mentorship Cohort Circle and Shining Stars for being a part of my community and for courageously sharing their gifts with the world.

My Right-Brain Business Plan licensed facilitators for being ambassadors of the work and for spreading the message farther than I ever could do on my own.

My in-laws Edmond and Ling Ng for being extremely helpful with our two moves while I was busy writing.

My parents Curtis and Irene Lee for their love and support and for encouraging me to be uniquely me.

# Index

*Page numbers in italic type refer to illustrations.*

# About the Author

Photo by Portraits to the People

Jennifer Lee is the founder of Artizen Coaching and the bestselling author of *The Right-Brain Business Plan: A Creative, Visual Map for Success*, which has helped tens of thousands of entrepreneurs around the world launch their creative businesses.

Before pursuing her own passions full-time, she consulted for ten years for Fortune 500 companies such as Gap Inc., Accenture, and HP, helping leaders and organizations manage change. As a director of executive development for Gap Inc., she led onboarding and coaching programs for those at the level of vice president and above. She grew her coaching business in her spare time, and in 2006 Jennifer made the courageous leap from corporate America to living the life of her dreams.

Jennifer has been featured in the *Wall Street Journal, U.S. News & World Report, Entrepreneur, Whole Living, Family Circle,* and *Cloth Paper Scissors Studios*; in several books; on numerous radio shows; and on ABC7 TV. She has also partnered with Levenger to develop the Right-Brain Business Plan Circa Notebook.

Jennifer holds a BA in communication studies from UCLA and an MA in communication management from USC. Things that light her up include getting lost in a good book, indulging in a midday nap, painting up a storm, and hiking in the woods. She lives in the San Francisco Bay Area with her creative, rather left-brain husband and their sweet husky-Lab mix.

For creative inspiration and more information on Jennifer's programs and products visit her website: www.rightbrainbusinessplan.com.

# Join the Right-Brain Business Revolution

Photo by Stefanie Renée

## Right-Brain Business-Building Bundle

Want additional support on your entrepreneurial journey? Download your FREE Right-Brain Business-Building Bundle, which includes

- a special bonus MP3 guided visualization that will inspire you to share your creative gifts with the world
- a short video class to walk you through the Entrepreneurial Ecosystem exercise
- full-color PDFs of all the illustrated play sheets featured in this book

Grab your goodies at www.rightbrainbusinessplan.com/rbbiz.

Scan to download bundle.